Vagus Nerve & Polyvagal Theory Exposed

Accessing the Vagus Nerve and the Healing Power of a Healthy Brain-Gut Connection, Ease Gastroparesis, Trauma and Complex PTSD (CPTSD)

By Sharon Copeland

© **Copyright 2020 - All rights reserved.**

The content contained within this book may not be reproduced, duplicated, or transmitted without direct written permission from the author or the publisher.

Under no circumstances will any blame or legal responsibility be held against the publisher, or author, for any damages, reparation, or monetary loss due to the information contained within this book, either directly or indirectly.

Legal Notice

This book is Copyright protected. It is only for personal use. You cannot amend, distribute, sell, use, quote, or paraphrase any part, or the content within this book, without the consent of the author or publisher.

Disclaimer Notice

Please note the information contained within this document is for educational and entertainment purposes only. All effort has been executed to present accurate, up-to-date, reliable, complete information. No warranties of any kind are declared or implied. Readers acknowledge that the author is not engaged in the rendering of legal, financial, medical, or professional advice. The content within this book has been derived from various sources. Please consult a licensed professional before attempting any techniques outlined in this book.

Table of Contents

Introduction 8

Free Workbook 10

Your Free Gift 11

Chapter 1 13

What is the Vagus Nerve? 13

    Anatomical Course 14

    Function and structure 17

    What does the Vagus Nerve affect? 20

Chapter 2 22

Functions of the Vagus Nerve 22

    The Vasovagal Reflex 26

    The Vagus Nerve and the heart 26

    The Role of Vagus in the Autonomic Nervous System 26

    Vagus Nerve is a Connection between the Central and ENS 28

Chapter 3 33

The Polyvagal Theory 33

    Our three-part nervous system 33

    Trauma's effect on the central nervous system response 35

    Certain aspects of ventral vagal nerve functioning 36

    Getting the picture 37

Chapter 4 39

Healing PTSD with the Polyvagal Theory 39

    Adaptation as Survival 39

    The Polyvagal Theory 40

Attentional Response Bias 41

The Takeaway 42

Chapter 5 44

Vagus Nerve Dysfunctions 44

Vagus Nerve Damage 44

Vagus Nerve Disorders 45

Symptoms of Vagus Nerve Dysfunction 46

Chapter 6 49

The Vagus Nerve and the Digestive System 49

Gastroparesis 49

How Does The Vagus Nerve Support Every Aspect Of Digestion? ... 52

The Brain-Gut Connection 53

Conclusion 58

Chapter 7 59

Immune Activation and Inflammation 59

The inflammatory reflex 60

Vagus Nerve in metabolic regulation 63

The inflammatory reflex and obesity 66

Conclusions 68

How is your reading going? 70

Free Workbook 71

Chapter 8 72

Overcome Stress with the Vagus Nerve 72

The Vagus Nerve being the Key to our Well-being. 75

The Role of the Vagus Nerve in Stress Management 76

Chapter 9 82

The Role of the Vagus Nerve in Social Engagements 82

Polyvagal Theory and just how It Relates to Social Cues 86

Peripheral Nervous System 87

The Vagus Nerve 88

Neuroception 89

3 Developmental Stages of Response 90

The Response Hierarchy in Life that is daily 91

Impact of Trauma 91

Connection and Polyvagal Theory 92

Chapter 10 94

Sleep Problems and the Vagus Nerve 94

Vagus Nerve Science for a much better Night's Sleep 94

Sleep deprivation 97

Tone Your Vagus Nerve to Sleep Better 99

Your Vagus Nerve 99

Heart Rate Variability 100

Resonant Frequency Breath Training 101

Paced Breathing to Induce Sleep 104

Take-Home Points 106

Chapter 11 108

Activating the Vagus Nerve 108

When to See a Doctor 108

Factors that could Stimulate the Vagus Nerve 109

Takeaway 124

Chapter 12 125

Treating the Vagus Nerve 125

Vagus Nerve Treatment Through Acupuncture 127

Treating the Vagus Nerve Through Mind-Body Therapy 128

Vagal Tone and Heart Rate Variability 129

Tone Your Vagus Nerve... 129

Conclusion 130

This is Not the End 132

Free Workbook 133

Introduction

The vagus nerve represents the parasympathetic nervous system's primary element, which oversees a wide array of crucial bodily functions, including control of mood, digestion, immune response, and heart rate. It establishes among the connections between the mind and the gastrointestinal tract and sends info about the state of the internal organs to the brain via afferent fibers. This book discusses several functions of the vagus nerve, making it an appealing target in treating gastrointestinal and psychiatric disorders. There's preliminary evidence that vagus nerve stimulation is a promising add-on treatment for treatment-refractory depression, inflammatory bowel disease, and post-traumatic stress disorder. Treatments that target the vagus nerve increases the vagal tone and inhibit cytokine production. Both are an important system of flexibility. The stimulation of vagal sensory fibers in the gut affects monoaminergic brain systems in the brain stem that play essential functions in major psychiatric conditions, like stress and anxiety and state of mind disorders. In line, there's preliminary evidence for gut bacteria to have a beneficial effect on anxiety and mood, partly by affecting the activity of the vagus nerve. Since the vagal tone is correlated with the capacity to regulate stress reactions and may be affected by breathing, its increase through meditation and yoga will likely contribute to resilience and the mitigation of mood and anxiety symptoms.

The bidirectional communication between the mind and also the gastrointestinal tract, the so-called "brain-gut axis," is based on a complicated system, like the vagus nerve, but also sympathetic (e.g., via the prevertebral ganglia), immune, endocrine, and humoral links also the influence of gut microbiota to be able to regulate gastrointestinal homeostasis and to connect cognitive and emotional areas of the brain with gut functions. The ENS produces much more than thirty neurotransmitters and has a lot more neurons than the spinal column. Peptides and hormones that the ENS releases into the blood circulation cross the blood-brain barrier (e.g., ghrelin) and also can act synergistically with the vagus nerve, for instance, to regulate appetite and food intake. The brain-gut axis is becoming crucial as a therapeutic target for psychiatric and gastrointestinal disorders, like inflammatory bowel disease (IBD), depression, and post-traumatic stress disorder (PTSD). The gut is a crucial control center of the immune system, and the vagus nerve has immunomodulatory properties. As a result, this nerve plays a crucial role in the relationship between inflammation, the brain, and the gut. You will find brand new treatment options for modulating the brain-gut axis, for instance, vagus nerve stimulation (VNS) and meditation methods. These treatments have been proven to be advantageous in anxiety and mood disorders and other conditions associated with increased inflammation. Particularly, gut-directed hypnotherapy was found to work in both irritable bowel syndrome and IBD. Finally, the vagus nerve also represents a crucial link between nutrition and psychiatric, inflammatory, and neurological diseases.

In order to maximize the value you receive from this book, you can also get in touch with me at the following contacts:

Website
sharoncopeland.com

Email
info@sharoncopeland.com

Facebook Page
https://swiy.io/SharonCopelandFBPage

Facebook Support Group:
https://swiy.io/SharonCopelandFBGroup

Instagram
@saroncopelandauthor

Get in touch with me for any feedback or question, I can't wait to hear from you soon!

Free Workbook

To help you take some "me" time and reflect on which actions to take after the reading, I have prepared a workbook with some key questions to ask yourself. I hope this helps!

You can find the workbook at the following link.

https://swiy.io/VagusNerveWorkbookLP

Or Scan This Code With your Phone Camera

Your Free Gift

You read it right! There is a second book waiting for you!

What is the cost? Zero! (0 $/€/£) or any currency you would usually pay with. :)

As a way of saying thanks for purchasing my book, I decided to offer you access to a FREE copy of my book.

Self-Help is a way to enhance our own spiritual and physical power. Self-Help is key to living a positive life and goes hand in hand with Empath. I consider it to be a good, complimentary reading for empaths, who want to take back self-control and more in general, want to get a better understanding of some self-help techniques.

https://swiy.io/selfhelpfree

MY OTHER BOOKS

Empath: Healing People with Positive Energy is a Gift. Master Your Emotions and Set Sensitive Boundaries to Empower Cognitive, Emotional, and Compassionate Empathy

Vagus Nerve & Polyvagal Theory Exposed: Accessing the Nervus Vagus and the Healing Power of a Healthy Brain-Gut Connection, Ease Gastroparesis, Trauma and Complex PTSD (CPTSD)

MY AUTHOR PAGE

https://swiy.io/SharonCopelandAmzAuthorPage

And now...Hope you enjoy the gift! Happy reading!

Sharon

Chapter 1

What is the Vagus Nerve?

The vagus nerve connects the brain to nearly all of the body's important organs, running from the brain stem down each side of the neck, across the chest, and into the abdomen. It's linked directly to two regions known to play roles in consciousness and alertness in the brain.

Various researchers have also identified that the vagus nerve controls glucose homeostasis, independent of insulin (via leptin). At any rate, it works that way in non-diabetics.

The vagus nerve, a cranial nerve, also runs from the brainstem to the abdomen and is liable for talking with our nervous system to turn on our bodies' parasympathetic nervous system, or perhaps relaxation feedback. When the vagus nerve is stimulated, it unleashes the neurotransmitter acetylcholine. Acetylcholine is accountable for learning and memory. It's also soothing and relaxing, which can be used by the vagus nerve to send messages of relaxation and peace throughout your body. The latest studies have found that acetylcholine is a major brake on inflammation in the body.

The vagus nerve contains two bunches of sensory nerve cell bodies, and it also connects the brainstem to the body. It enables the brain to monitor and receive info about a number of the body's various functions.

You will discover several nerve system works supplied by the vagus nerve and its involved parts. The vagus nerve functions contribute to the free nerve system, including parasympathetic and considerate parts.

The nerve is accountable for some sensory-motor and activity info for movement within the body.

It's an element of a circuit that links the neck, lungs, heart, and abdomen to the human brain.

You will find twelve cranial nerves within the body. They are available in help and pairs to link the brain with other parts of the body, like the head, neck, and torso.

Some send sensory info, including details about smells, sights, tastes, and sounds, to the human brain. These nerves are referred to as having sensory functions. Other cranial nerves control the motion of the performance and different muscles of certain glands. These are known as motor functions.

While some cranial nerves have either sensory or perhaps motor functions, others have both. The vagus nerve is such a nerve. The cranial nerves are classified using Roman numerals based on their area. The vagus nerve can also be called cranial nerve X.

Anatomical Course

The vagus nerve has probably the longest course of all cranial nerves, extending from the head to the abdomen. Its name is derived from the Latin vagary--meaning wandering. It's at times called the wandering nerve.

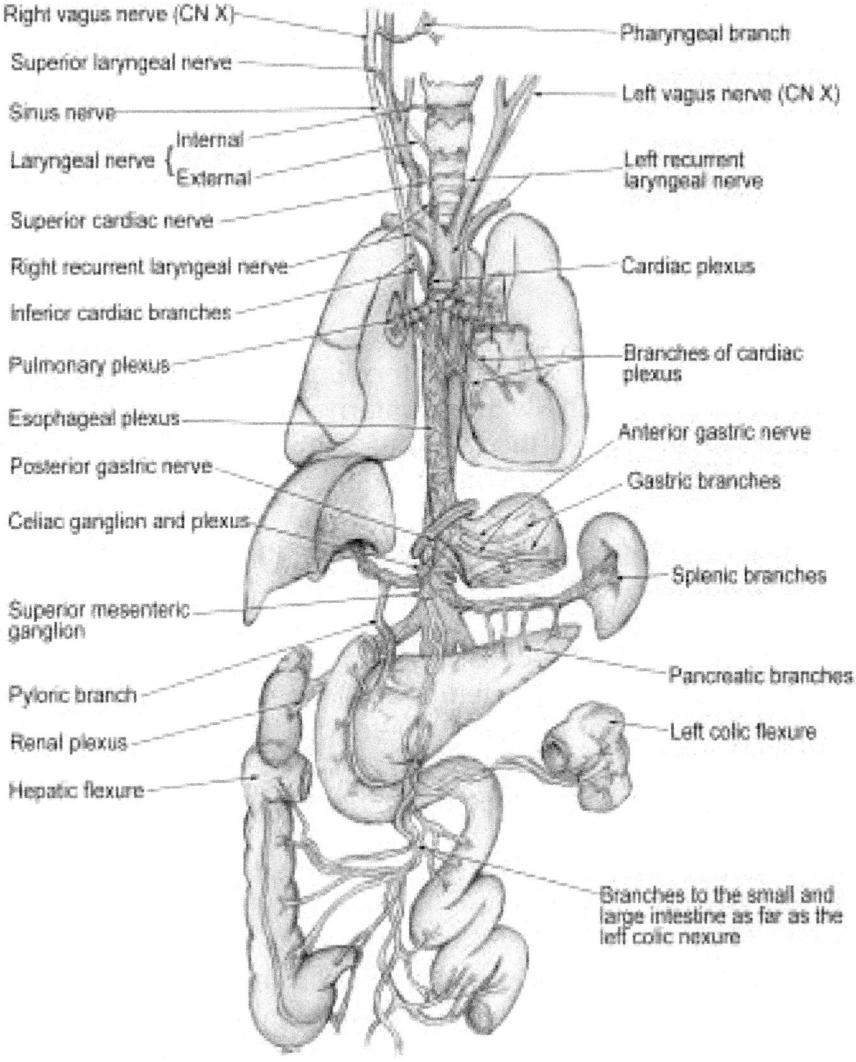
Right vagus nerve (CN X)
Superior laryngeal nerve
Sinus nerve
Laryngeal nerve
Internal
External
Superior cardiac nerve
Right recurrent laryngeal nerve
Inferior cardiac branches
Pulmonary plexus
Esophageal plexus
Posterior gastric nerve
Celiac ganglion and plexus
Superior mesenteric ganglion
Pyloric branch
Renal plexus
Hepatic flexure
Pharyngeal branch
Left vagus nerve (CN X)
Left recurrent laryngeal nerve
Cardiac plexus
Branches of cardiac plexus
Anterior gastric nerve
Gastric branches
Splenic branches
Pancreatic branches
Left colic flexure
Branches to the small and large intestine as far as the left colic nexure

In the Head

The vagus nerve springs from the medulla of the brainstem. It withdraws from the skull through the jugular foramen, with the glossopharyngeal and accessory nerves.

Within the skull, the auricular branch arises. This supplies sensation to the posterior portion of the external auditory canal and external ear.

In the Neck

The vagus nerve enters the carotid sheath in the neck, traveling inferiorly with the internal jugular vein and common carotid artery. At the bottom of the neck, the right and left nerves have differing pathways:

The right vagus nerve passes anterior to the subclavian artery and posterior to the sternoclavicular joint, going into the thorax.

The left vagus nerve passes inferiorly between the left common carotid and left subclavian arteries, posterior to the sternoclavicular joint, going into the thorax.

Several branches come up in the neck:

Pharyngeal branches-- provides motor innervation to the vast majority of the soft palate muscles and the pharynx.

Superior laryngeal nerve-- splits into external and internal branches. The external laryngeal nerve innervates the cricothyroid muscle of the larynx. The internal laryngeal provides sensory innervation to the better part and the laryngopharynx of the larynx.

Recurrent laryngeal nerve (the side that is right only)-- hooks underneath the right subclavian artery ascends towards the larynx. It triggers most of the intrinsic muscles of the larynx.

In the Thorax

In the thorax, the right vagus nerve forms the posterior vagal trunk, so the left forms the anterior vagal trunk. Branches from the vagal trunks contribute to developing the oesophageal plexus, which innervates the esophagus' smooth muscle.

Two different branches come up in the thorax:

Left recurrent laryngeal nerve-- it hooks under the aorta arch, ascending to innervate the vast majority of the larynx's intrinsic muscles.

Cardiac branches-- these regulate heart rate and provide visceral sensation to the organ.

The vagal trunks enter the abdomen via the oesophageal hiatus, an opening in the diaphragm.

In the Abdomen

In the abdomen, the vagal trunks terminate by dividing into branches that supply the oesophagus, stomach, and the large and small bowel (up to the splenic flexure).

Function and structure

As mentioned earlier, the vagus nerve has its origin in the medulla oblongata and exits the skull through the jugular foramen. You will discover two ganglia on the vagus nerve (inferior and superior). It withdraws from the jugular foramen; the spinal accessory nerve joins the vagus nerve simply distal to the inferior ganglion.

The emergence of cell bodies for the vagus nerve comes from the nucleus ambiguous, the dorsal motor nucleus of X (vagus nerve), the exceptional ganglion of X, and X's inferior ganglion. The nerve fibers from the nucleus ambiguous are efferent, special visceral (ESV) fibers, which help mediate phonation and swallowing. Fibers from the dorsal motor nucleus of X are efferent, general visceral (EGV) fibers, which provide the uncontrolled muscle control of organs it innervates (heart, lung, esophageal) and stimulation to glands throughout the gastrointestinal tract. The vagus nerve's superior ganglion provides afferent general somatic innervation to the external ear and tympanic membrane. X's inferior ganglion supplies afferent basic visceral fibers to aortic bodies and the carotid; the efferent fibers of this nerve travel to the nucleus tractus solitarius; the inferior ganglion likewise supplies taste feeling to the pharynx and relays this info to the nucleus tractus solitarius.

The vagus nerve continues by taking a trip inferiorly within the carotid sheath precisely where it's situated posterior and lateral to the internal and common carotid arteries and medial to the internal jugular vein. The right vagus nerve takes a trip anteriorly to the subclavian artery then posterior to the innominate artery. It makes its fall into the thoracic cavity by travelling to the right of the trachea, and posterior to the hilum on the right, moving medially to form the esophageal plexus with the left angus Nerve. The left vagus nerve takes a trip anteriorly to the subclavian artery and goes into the thoracic cavity wedged between the left typical carotid and subclavian arteries. After that, it comes down posteriorly to the phrenic nerve and posterior to the left lung, then travels medially towards the esophagus, structuring the esophageal plexus with the right vagus nerve.

You will find four branches of the vagus nerve within the neck: pharyngeal branches, superior laryngeal nerve, recurrent laryngeal nerve, and the superior cardiac nerve.

The pharyngeal nerve branches emerge from the vagus nerve's inferior ganglion, containing both motor and sensory fibers. These fibers shape the pharyngeal plexus-branches of this plexus stimulate the pharyngeal and palate muscles (except the tensor palatine muscle); the pharyngeal plexus also supplies the innervation to the intercarotid plexus, which mediates information from the carotid body.

The superior laryngeal nerve travels between the internal and external carotid arteries; the nerve divides into external and internal branches near the hyoid's amount. The inner laryngeal nerve goes through the thyrohyoid membrane launching to the larynx. The outside portion travels distally with the superior thyroid vessels. The outside portion supplies the cricothyroid muscle, whereas the internal branch supplies the mucosa better than the glottis.

The right laryngeal nerve's fibers branch from the vagus nerve near the right subclavian artery, traveling superiorly to the larynx between the cricopharyngeus muscle well as the esophagus. The left laryngeal nerve then loops around the aortic arch distal to the ligamentum arteriosus, after which enters the larynx. All the laryngeal musculatures receive supply via the recurrent laryngeal nerve except for the cricothyroid muscle (supplied by the laryngeal nerve).

While the vagus nerve is within the carotid sheath, it releases the remarkable cardiac nerve related to parasympathetic fibers and travels to the heart.

The vagus nerve emits posterior and anterior bronchial branches in which the anterior branches are along the anterior lung forming the anterior pulmonary plexus. On the other hand, the posterior branches form the posterior lung plexus.

Esophageal branches of the vagus nerve are anterior and posterior and form the esophageal plexus. The left vagus is anterior to the esophagus; the right vagus is posterior.

Stomach branches supply the stomach; celiac branches (primarily stemmed from the right vagus nerve) supply the pancreas, adrenals, kidneys, spleen, and small intestine.

What does the vagus nerve affect?

The vagus nerve has different purposes. The vagus nerve's four main functions are sensory: from the throat, lungs, heart, and abdomen. Special sensory where it provides taste sensation behind the tongue. Motor, where it provides movement functions for the muscles in the neck responsible for swallowing and speech.
And parasympathetic, which is responsible for the intestinal tract, heart rate functioning, and respiration.

Its functions can be broken down further into more categories. One of them is balancing the nervous system.

The nervous system may be divided into two areas: parasympathetic and sympathetic. The sympathetic side increases alertness, breathing rate, blood pressure, heart rate, and energy.

The parasympathetic part, which the vagus nerve is highly involved in, decreases alertness, blood pressure, and heart rate and helps relaxation, digestion, and calmness. As an outcome, the vagus nerve also helps with sexual arousal, urination, and defecation.

Other vagus nerve effects include:

Communication between the gut and the brain: The vagus nerve delivers info from the gut to the human brain.

Relaxation with breathing: The vagus nerve communicates with the diaphragm. With deep breaths, a person feels a lot calmer.

Decreasing inflammation: The vagus nerve signals an anti-inflammatory warning to other areas of the body.

Lowering the blood pressure and heart rate: If the vagus nerve is overactive, it can result in the heart being unable to pump enough blood around the body. In several cases, excessive vagus nerve activity can result in loss of consciousness and organ damage.

Fear management: The vagus nerve sends information from the gut to the brain associated with dealing with stress, anxiety, and fear-- hence the saying, gut feeling. These signals help an individual to recover from scary and stressful situations.

Chapter 2

Functions of the Vagus Nerve

The vagus nerve has probably the most extensive distribution of all of the cranial nerves. It has two nerves, ranging from the brain stem and branching out through the neck and down each side of the body, throughout the abdominal location, and the main organs.

As a result, the extremely intricate circuitry that comprises the whole vagus nerve functions in myriad physical functions, including breathing, maintaining the digestive function, and keeping track of the heartbeat to guarantee that it stays in a regular rhythm. When we are hungry or feel our chest tighten, it's the vagus nerve duty to relay the message. The vagus nerve also transmits sensory information from the ear, throat, tongue, windpipe, and voice box.

Just like the nerve itself, vagus nerve disorders are usually also called 10th cranial nerve disorders. These disorders can have several different impacts that are as complicated as the nerve itself, although some effects are certainly more typical compared to others.

For instance, if the vagus nerve is stimulated, or even if it's compressed, the outcome is usually unconsciousness, crisp skin, and/or nausea. When stimulated, the vagus nerve can cause the heart to relax and drop blood pressure levels. While this may seem to be damaging in numerous cases, the vagus nerve is often stimulated to treat people suffering from severe depression and epilepsy

The vagus nerve's biggest significance is supplying parasympathetic fibers to each of the principal organs of the head, neck, abdomen, and chest. The vagus nerve is accountable for the gag reflex (and the cough reflex when the ear canal is stimulated), slowing the heart rate, controlling sweating, regulating blood pressure, and stimulating the gastrointestinal tract's peristalsis, and controlling vascular tone.

Vagus nerve function is divided into four groups based on the type of nerve fiber: sensory, motor, special sensory, and parasympathetic. Although mostly an afferent nerve that brings sensory details from the body to the brain, the vagus nerve is an efferent (motor) nerve that brings messages from the brain to muscle. The parasympathetic nervous system controls smooth muscle control.

Four separate vagal passageways exit from the medulla oblongata:

Dorsal nucleus: sends parasympathetic information to the viscera

Solitary nucleus: receives sensory info from the tongue (visceral organs and taste)

Spinal or back trigeminal nucleus: receives sensory information from the outer ear and laryngeal mucosa

Ambiguous nucleus: motor nerve related to swallowing, speech, and heart muscle activity.

Cranial nerve nuclei are gray matter found in the brainstem and stand for the synapse's effort. Neurons are exiting the vagus nerve in the medulla oblongata's first synapse in their associated nuclei before continuing to different locations in the body. In the same way, messages sent to the brain from other fractions of the body synapse at the nuclei before their words reach the medulla oblongata.

The vagus nerve (being the sensory nerve) innervates the skin and mucous membranes of the external ear, throat (laryngopharynx), and voice box (throat). It also provides visceral sensation in visceral organs that allow an individual to feel pain, vibration, distension, and nausea. For instance, the nerve also sends involuntary signals in reaction to certain chemical stimuli- hormones and neurotransmitters. The visceral organs include the heart, pancreas, liver, lungs, and intestines.

As a unique sensory nerve (where "unique" describes the senses of smell, hearing, taste, vision, and proprioception), the vagus nerve collects information from the feeling buds of the upper epiglottis and the tongue. CN X, as a motor nerve, triggers the muscles of the throat.

The parasympathetic nervous system has a spontaneous resting function, which brings the body to a calmer state after the considerate battle. Flight reaction is not required for survival. The vagus nerve is an element of the parasympathetic nervous system and innervates the heart's smooth muscle, trachea, bronchi of the lungs, and gastrointestinal system. It will make the heart rate and breathing rate sluggish and increase gut peristalsis if promoted.

WHAT THE VAGUS NERVE DOES

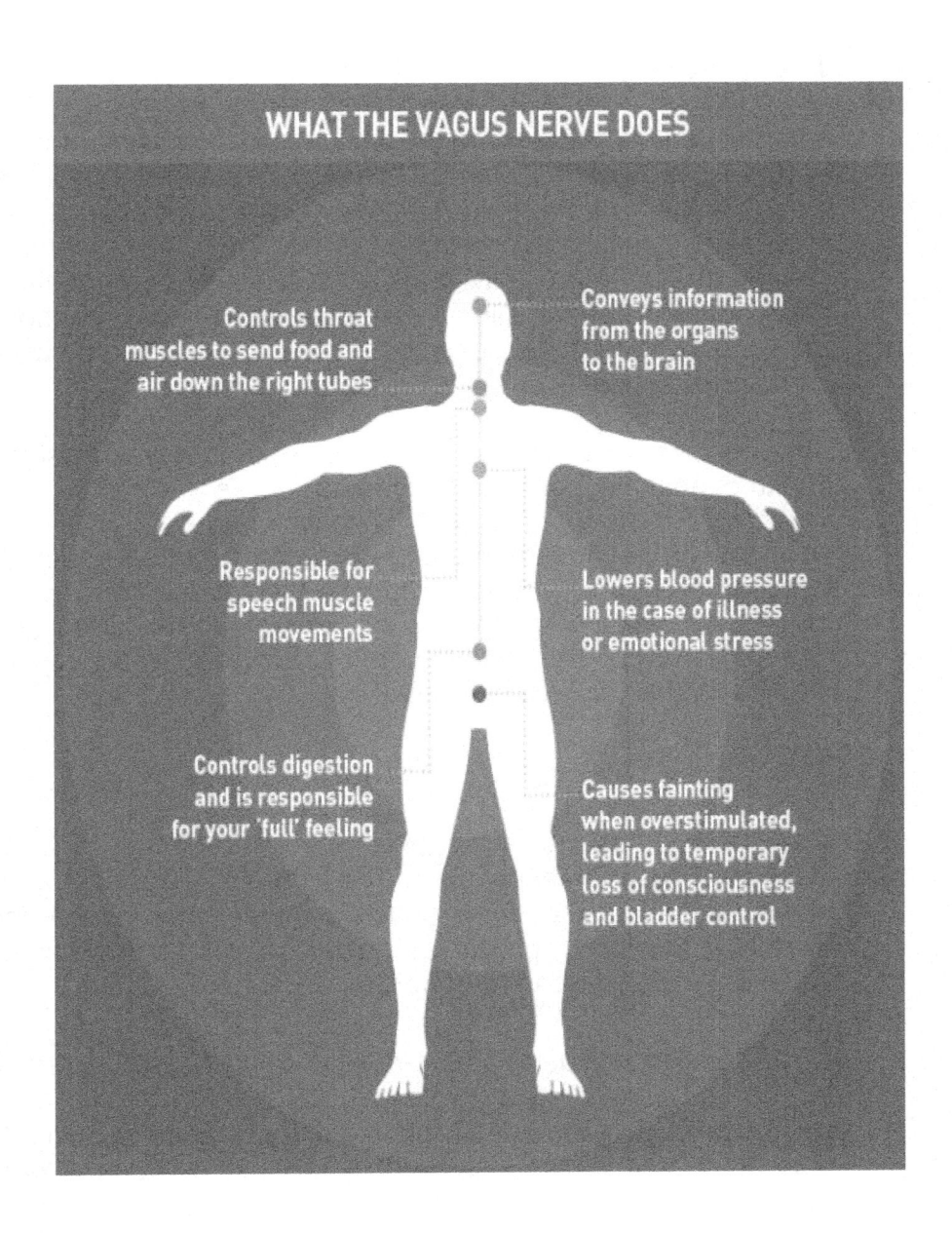

Controls throat muscles to send food and air down the right tubes

Conveys information from the organs to the brain

Responsible for speech muscle movements

Lowers blood pressure in the case of illness or emotional stress

Controls digestion and is responsible for your 'full' feeling

Causes fainting when overstimulated, leading to temporary loss of consciousness and bladder control

The Vasovagal Reflex

A vagus nerve's sudden stimulation can produce what's known as a "vasovagal reflex," which consists of a sudden drop in the blood pressure of the heart rate. This reflex can be caused by gastrointestinal illness or perhaps in reaction to pain, fright, or sudden stress. Many individuals are especially susceptible to vasovagal reflex. Their blood pressure and heart rate changes can result in loss of consciousness - a condition called "vasovagal syncope."

Abnormal activation of the vagus nerve is observed in some health conditions, particularly dysautonomias.

Stimulating the vagus nerve can have healing effects such as stopping episodes of supraventricular tachycardia (hiccups or SVT) and could help doctors diagnose specific heart-type murmurs. Vagal stimulation can be achieved relatively by employing the valsalva maneuver.

The Vagus Nerve and the Heart

The right vagus nerve supplies the sinus node, and its stimulation can produce sinus bradycardia. The left vagus nerve provides the AV node, and its stimulus can create a kind of heart block. It is by producing a transient heart block that the valsalva maneuver can terminate.

The Role of Vagus in the Autonomic Nervous System

Along with the supportive nerve system and the enteric nervous system (ENS), the parasympathetic nervous system represents the free nerve system's three branches.

The meaning of the sympathetic and parasympathetic nervous systems is primarily anatomical. The vagus nerve will be the major contributor to the parasympathetic nervous system. The other three parasympathetic cranial nerves are the nervus oculomotorius, the nervus glossopharyngeus, and the nervus facialis.

The vagus nerve's most crucial feature is afferent, bringing information of the internal organs, such as the gut, heart, liver, and lungs, to the human brain. This implies that the internal organs are significant sources of sensory info to the human mind. The gut is probably the most extensive surface toward the external world and might be an especially crucial sensory part of the body.

Generally, the vagus has been studied as an eccentric nerve and a sympathetic nervous system's villain. Most organs receive parasympathetic divergence through the vagus nerve and understanding efferents through the splanchnic nerves. Together with the delicate nervous systems, the parasympathetic nervous system is accountable for regulating vegetative functions by opposing one another. The parasympathetic innervation causes dilatation of bronchioles and capillary and stimulation of salivary glands. On the contrary, the considerate innervation results in a constriction of the capillary, a dilatation of bronchioles, a rise in heart rate, and a tightness of the digestive tract and urinary sphincters. In the intestinal tract, the activation of the parasympathetic nervous system increases glandular secretion and bowel motility. In contrast to it, the understanding activity reduces a reduction and digestive activity of blood flow to the gut, enabling higher blood circulation to the muscles and the heart, as soon as it faces existential stress.

The ENS emerges from the vagal origin's neural crest cells and includes a nerve plexus embedded in the intestinal tract wall, extending across the entire intestinal tract from the esophagus to the anus. It's believed that the human ENS contains approximately 100-500 million neurons. This is probably the most significant accumulation of nerve cells in the body. Since the ENS is akin to the brain regarding chemical coding, function, or structure, it's been referred to as the second brain or perhaps the mind within the gut. It consists of two ganglionated plexuses - the submucosal plexus manages gastrointestinal blood flow, controls the epithelial cell secretion and function, and the myenteric plexus regulates the relaxation and contraction of the digestive wall. The ENS acts as a digestive tract barrier and controls the significant enteric procedures, such as immune action, identifying nutrients, motility, microvascular flow, and epithelial secretion of fluids, ions, and bioactivity peptides. There is communication between the vagal nerve and the ENS, and the primary transmitter is cholinergic activation through nicotinic receptors. The interaction of ENS and the vagal nerve as parts of the CNS leads to a bidirectional flow of information.

On the contrary, the ENS in the big and small bowel can also work extremely separate from vagal control. It contains complete reflex circuits, including sensory, motor, and nerve cells. They manage muscle activity and motility, fluid fluxes, mucosal blood circulation, and the mucosal barrier function. ENS nerve cells will likewise remain in close contact with cells of the inherent and adaptive immune system and manage their activities and services. Cell lobe ENS are related to grievances such as incontinence and constipation. The failure of the ENS in the large and little intestinal tract could be dangerous (Hirschsprung's disease; pseudo intestinal tract blockage), whereas loss of the vagal nerve in these places is not.

Vagus Nerve is a Connection between the Central and ENS

The relationship between the ENS and CNS (also known as the brain-gut axis) enables the bidirectional connection between the mind and the gastrointestinal tract. It's responsible for monitoring the physiological homeostasis and connecting the brain's cognitive and emotional areas with peripheral intestinal functions, like immune activation, enteric reflex, intestinal permeability, and enteroendocrine signaling.

This brain-gut axis consists of the brain, the spinal cord, the free nervous system (supportive, parasympathetic, and ENS), and the hypothalamic pituitary adrenal (HPA) axis. The vagal efferents send the signals below the brain to the gut through efferent fibers, which account for 10-20 % of all the threads, and the vagal afferents up from the digestive wall to the brain accounting for 80-90 % of all fibers. The vagal afferent pathways are associated with the activation/regulation of the HPA axis, which coordinates the organism's adaptive responses to stressors of any kind. Environmental stress and elevated systemic proinflammatory cytokines activate the HPA axis through secretion of the corticotropin-releasing factor (CRF) from the hypothalamus. The CRF releases adrenocorticotropic hormone (ACTH) secretion from the pituitary gland. This stimulation, in turn, causes cortisol release from the adrenal glands. Cortisol is a substantial tension hormone that affects many human organs, like the brain, muscles, bones, and body fat.

Both hormonal and neural lines of communication combine to allow the brain to affect intestinal functional effector cells' activities, like immune cells, epithelial cells, enteric neurons, smooth muscle interstitial cells of Cajal enterochromaffin cells. These cells, on the contrary, are under the influence of gut microbiota. The gut microbiota has a considerable result on the brain-gut axis, communicating not just with intestinal cells and ENS but also by directly impacting metabolic systems and neuroendocrine. Surfacing data support the role of microbiota in shaping stress and anxiety and depressive-like behaviors. Research conducted on germ-free animals demonstrated that microbiota influences stress reactivity and anxiety-like behavior and regulate the set point for HPA activity. Consequently, these animals commonly show decreased anxiety and increased stress response with augmented cortisol and ACTH levels.

In food intake, vagal afferents innervating the gastrointestinal tract provide a discrete and rapid account of digestible food and circulating saved fuels While vagal efferents together with the hormonal systems, codetermine the rate of nutrient mobilization, absorption, and storage. Electrophysiological and histological evidence indicates that visceral afferent endings of the Vagus Nerve in the intestinal tract express a diverse range of chemical and mechanosensitive receptors. These receptors are targets of regulatory peptides and gut hormonal agents released from enteroendocrine cells of the intestinal system in response to nutrients through distension of the stomach and neuronal signals. They affect the control of food intake and policy of satiety, gastric emptying, and energy balance by transmitting signals occurring from the top of the gut to the nucleus of the solitary system in the human brain. Like peptide cholecystokinin (leptin, ghrelin, and CCK), many of these hormones are vulnerable to the gut's nutrient content. They are involved in regulating short term feelings of satisfaction and hunger.

Cholecystokinin controls gastrointestinal functions, including inhibition of stomach emptying and food intake through activation of CCK 1 receptors on vagal afferent fibers innervating the gut. Additionally, CCK is essential for the secretion of pancreatic fluid and producing gastric acid, contracting the gallbladder, decreasing gastric emptying, and facilitating digestion. Saturated fat, long-chain fats, amino acids, and small peptides from protein digestion stimulate CCK's liberation from the small intestine. You will find many biologically active forms of CCK, classified based on the variety of amino acids they contain, CCK-22, CCK-8, CCK-5, i.e., and CCK 33. In neurons, CCK 8 is for sure the predominating form.

In contrast, the endocrine gut cells contain a combination of more significant and small CCK peptides, of which CCK 22 or CCK 33 often dominate. In rats, long and short-chain fatty acids from food activate jejunal vagal afferent nerve fibers but do this through distinct mechanisms. Short-chain fats, for example, butyric acid, have an instant result on vagal afferent terminals while the long-chain fatty acids activate vagal afferents by a CCK dependent system. The exogenous administration of CCK seems to prevent endogenous CCK secretion. CCK is contained in enteric vagal afferent neurons, in the cerebral cortex, in the thalamus, hypothalamus, basal ganglia, and dorsal hindbrain and works as a neurotransmitter. It activates vagal afferent terminals in the NTS by increasing calcium release.

Additionally, there's proof that CCK can activate neurons in the hindbrain and myenteric intestinal plexus (a plexus which provides motor innervation to both levels of the muscular level of the gut) in rats. That capsaicin or vagotomy treatment leads to an attenuation of CCK induced Fos expression (a proto-oncogene) in the brain. There's also considerable evidence that elevated levels of CCK cause feelings of anxiety. Therefore, CCK is a difficult agent to model stress and anxiety disorders in animals and people.

Ghrelin is another hormone released into the blood circulation from the stomach and plays a vital function in promoting food consumption by preventing a vagal afferent shooting. Flowing ghrelin levels are increased by fasting and fall after a meal. Peripheral or central administration of acylated ghrelin to rats acutely stimulates food consumption and growth hormone release, and chronic administration causes weight gain. The ghrelin's feeding action is eliminated or perhaps attenuated in rats that have gone through treatment or vagotomy with capsaicin, a particular afferent neurotoxin. In humans, subcutaneous injection or perhaps intravenous infusion increases both hunger and food intake feelings since ghrelin suppresses insulin release. Thus, it's not surprising that secretion is disturbed in obesity as well as insulin resistance.

Leptin receptors are also identified in the vagus nerve. Studies in rodents indicate that leptin and CCK interact synergistically to induce short term inhibition of long term reduction and food intake of body weight. The epithelial cells that answer to both ghrelin and leptin lie near the vagal mucosal endings and modulate vagal afferents' activity, acting in concert to handle food consumption. After diet-induced obesity and fasting in mice, leptin loses its potentiating influence on vagal mucosal afferents.

The gastrointestinal tract will be the critical interface between food and the human body and can similarly sense basic tastes as the tongue through similar G-protein-coupled taste receptors. Various taste qualities induce the release of different gastric peptides. Bitter taste receptors can be viewed as potential targets to lower appetite by promoting the release of CCK. Furthermore, activation of bitter taste receptors promotes ghrelin secretion and, consequently, impacts the vagus nerve.

Chapter 3

The Polyvagal Theory

Imagining brain chemistry can be something like picturing a cyclone. We can imagine lousy weather, and it's challenging to envision changing the climate. Stephen Porges' polyvagal theory offers therapists a helpful picture of the neurological system, which might direct us in our attempts to assist customers. The vagus nerve serves the parasympathetic nerve system, an enjoyable aspect of our nerve system mechanics. The parasympathetic part of the free nerve system stabilizes the supportive, active role in more nuanced methods than we understood before the polyvagal theory.

Our three-part nervous system

Before polyvagal theory, our central nervous system was pictured as a two-part antagonistic system, with more activation signaling less calming and more relaxing, signaling less activation. The polyvagal theory acknowledges a third type of central nervous system action that Porges calls the social engagement system, a playful mix of activation and relaxation that operates out of remarkable nerve impact.

The social engagement system assists us in navigating relationships. Helping our customers to use their social engagement system permits them to be flexible in their coping styles.

The two other areas of our central nervous system function to help us manage life-threatening situations. Most counselors are acquainted with the two defense mechanisms triggered by these two tense system areas: sympathetic fight-or-flight and parasympathetic shutdown. The use of our social engagement system, on the other hand, involves a sense of security.

Polyvagal theory assists us in understanding that both branches of the vagus nerve relax the body. However, they do this in ways that are different. Shutdown, or maybe freeze-or-faint, takes place through the dorsal branch of the vagus nerve. This response can feel like the tired muscles and lightheadedness of awful influenza. When the dorsal vagal nerve closes down the body, it can move us into dissociation or immobility. The dorsal branch impacts the body functioning below the diaphragm and is involved in digestive concerns and impacting the heart and lungs.

The forward branch of the vagal nerve impacts the body working above the diaphragm. This is the branch that benefits the social engagement system. The forward vagal nerve moistens the body's regularly active state. Imagine controlling a horse as you ride it to the steady. You will continue to push back and release the reins in nuanced ways to ensure that the horse maintains a superior speed. Furthermore, the ventral vagal nerve allows activation subtly, therefore offering another quality than sympathetic activation.

Forward vagal release into activity takes milliseconds, whereas understanding activation takes seconds and involves numerous chain reactions comparable to losing the horse's reins. Additionally, after the fight-or-flight chemical reactions have begun, our bodies can get 10-20 minutes to go back to our pre-fight/pre-flight state. Ventral vagal release into activity doesn't involve these kinds of chemical reactions. Consequently, we can make quick adjustments between activation and calming, much like we can do when using the reins to manage the horse.

If you go to a dog park, you are going to see individual dogs that are scared. They exhibit fight-or-flight behaviors. Some other dogs are going to signal a wish to play. This signaling might take the form that we people hijacked for the downward-facing-dog pose in yoga. When a dog offers this signal, it cues a level of arousal, which can be extreme.

Nevertheless, this lively energy has various spirit than the intensity of fight-or-flight habits. This playful spirit defines the social engagement system. When we experience our environment as safe, we operate from our social engagement system.

Trauma's effect on the central nervous system response

If we have unresolved trauma in our past, we might live in a version of perpetual fight-or-flight. We might be ready to channel this fight-or-flight anxiety into activities like cleaning the house, raking the leaves, or even exercising at the gym. However, these activities can have a different experience than they would if they had been done with social engagement biology.

For many trauma survivors, no activity successfully channels their fight-or-flight sensations. The outcome was their bodies shut down and felt trapped. These clients may reside in a version of a perpetual shutdown.

Emerging from shutdown requires a shudder or perhaps shake to discharge suspended fight-or-flight energy. If we have shut down in a life-threatening situation and an opportunity for active survival presents itself, we can wake ourselves up. As counselors, we may recognize this shift from shutdown to fight-or-flight in a client's move from depression into anxiety.

But can we help our clients move into their social engagement biology? If clients live in a dissociative, depressed, and shutdown manner, we should help them shift temporarily into fight-or-flight. As clients experience fight-or-flight intensity, we should next help them find a sense of security. When they can sense they're safe, they can shift into their social engagement system.

The body awareness strategies, which belong to cognitive behavior modification (dialectical habits and CBT) treatment (DBT), can help clients pull out dissociative, shutdown responses by motivating them to be embodied. When clients are more involved in their health and better positioned to attend to momentary muscular tension, they could wake up from a shutdown response. The thought restructuring techniques usually part of DBT and CBT can teach clients to evaluate their safety much more accurately as clients activate out of change and shut down toward fight-or-flight sensations. Reflective listening techniques can help make clients feel a connection with their counselors. This can make it easy for these clients to feel secure enough to shift into social engagement biology.

Certain aspects of ventral vagal nerve functioning

The name social engagement system was selected because the ventral vagal nerve affects the middle ear, removing background noises to make it simpler to get the human voice. Additionally, it affects facial muscles, and therefore, the capability to make communicative facial expressions. Lastly, it affects the larynx and vocal patterning, thus vocal tone, helping humans create sounds that soothe one another.

Clients with inferior social engagement system functioning may have inner ear struggles that make it difficult for them to get soothing from others' voices. As counselors, we can be mindful of our vocal patterns and facial expressions and interested in the effects those elements of our communication have on our clients.

Based on his knowledge of the vagus nerve's consequences, extending exhales longer compared to inhales for some time stimulates the parasympathetic nervous system.

As a dance therapist, I'm conscious that extending clients' exhales who are stuck in forms of the fight-or-flight response to go into a feeling of security. For clients stuck in some shutdown type, I've found that conscious breathwork can stir the fight-or-flight response. When this happens, the fight-or-flight energy needs to be discharged through movement for clients to get a sense of security. For example, these clients might have to run in place and punch a pillow. The hierarchy of defense system functioning describes these healing methods.

Respiratory sinus arrhythmia is an excellent index of ventral vagal functioning. What this means is we now have ways to study the effectiveness of expressive arts and body therapies.

Getting the picture

As therapists are equipped with the polyvagal theory, we can imagine the defense mechanism hierarchy. We can acknowledge shifts from fight-or-flight to shut down when clients feel trapped. Likewise, we can recognize the motion from shutdown into fight-or-flight that comes with a possible transition into social engagement biology if the client can gain a security feeling.

Before the polyvagal theory, many counselors could most likely recognize fight-or-flight and shutdown behaviors. They can most likely notice a considerable difference between defense actions designed for dangerous situations and responses that identify the social engagement system. Polyvagal theory deepens the awareness that restorative surrender and lively arousal have a distinct nervous system impact.

Most counselors value brain science but may find it hard to picture how you can utilize the info. Because the polyvagal theory clarifies the vagus nerve's ventral branch, we now have a map to guide us.

Chapter 4

Healing PTSD with the Polyvagal Theory

If you've grown up with long-term, chronic trauma exposure, you may find it hard to accurately see whether folks or perhaps places are trustworthy or safe. At times, it may become hard to differentiate between experiences that happened in the past and what's going on today, in the current moment. The polyvagal theory helps us acknowledge the neural circuits involved in these signs of PSTD and brighten a course to flexibility.

The first research about stress and trauma identified the sympathetic nervous system as in charge of PTSD symptoms. As a result, symptom decrease highlighted accessing the parasympathetic nervous system's recovery power and the relaxation action. During this time, the parasympathetic nervous system was simply related to our ability to rest, restore, absorb, and heal from injury. While the parasympathetic nerve system does contribute to recovery, it is not the whole story.

Adaptation as Survival

If you've grown up in a chronically threatening environment, you most likely had to adapt to survive. Adaptations happen emotionally, behaviorally, and within the nervous system—these characteristics for complex PTSD (CPTSD). For instance, you may have carried toxic shame, learned to stay away from potentially hazardous situations, or perhaps dissociated when you could not escape. When served a crucial goal, all of these habits might have. Nevertheless, as adults, these same behaviors often create issues in your relationships, ability to parent kids, or perhaps to succeed in your work.

One key to healing from CPTSD is to develop self-compassion. The polyvagal theory teaches us that post-traumatic stress symptom are biologically based and somatically experienced. When you understand CPTSD symptoms' physiology, you realize exactly why you can't simply think your way out of your trauma reactions. While you may continue to repeat the actions that helped you survive, it's crucial to learn how to lean into yourself with love.

The Polyvagal Theory

The polyvagal theory explains three neural circuits that underlie various methods of working out with our surroundings. When we feel safe, we rely on a neural circuit that promotes social engagement behaviors. He calls this the social nervous system. This specific element of the parasympathetic nervous system engages neural structures that prevent our defensive systems. This relies upon the myelinated forward vagus nerve enabling us to engage socially by making eye contact, softening our voice tone, and revealing care with our face. The social nervous system can significantly facilitate immobilization within a safe context to promote higher intimacy or closeness.

At first, whenever we have a threat, we may well rely upon our social nervous system to resolve the situation. We could reach out for proximity or connection with another to re-establish safety. Nevertheless, if this is unsuccessful or if the risk is much more intense, we will begin to engage the sympathetic nervous system activation of flight or fight.

If we're not able to resolve the threatening situation by fighting or perhaps fleeing, then we are going to begin to engage an unmyelinated, evolutionarily older part of the vagus nerve to survive. This is particularly the case in circumstances that are life-threatening in which there's no escape. The dorsal vagal neural pathway is part of the parasympathetic nervous system; however, immobilization becomes a protective response. Usually, this is described as a weak response. Often, one can faint because the dorsal vagal pathway reduces blood flow on the human brain. Short of fainting, this defensive pathway can result in symptoms like dizziness, nausea, and fatigue, all signs of dissociation.

Your physiology not only holds the memories of trauma but likewise holds an important key to healing. The polyvagal theory points us towards another key to recover your capacity to engage the social nervous system. You can facilitate your social nervous system's health by establishing conscious awareness of your body's feelings, including your heart rate or possibly breath. This helps you recognize your signs of anxiety and allows you to respond instantly - before the stress feels overwhelming or perhaps out of your power.

Attentional Response Bias

Unfortunately, individuals with complex PTSD have a hard time orienting to safety even in situations in which there's no present threat. This is since it may be hard to differentiate between experiences that happened in the past and what's going on today, in the current moment. The past and present seem to get blurred because of the physiological alarm bells that continue to sound. This procedure is described as attentional threat bias, a factor that provides and exacerbates post-traumatic stress conditions.

Attentional response bias accounts for the more chance that people with PTSD perceive neutral faces as fearful and aggressive faces as angry. Moreover, after a threat has been perceived, these individuals often have trouble disengaging from such stimuli. In other terms, they perseverate on the perceived threat, and it gets a lot more and harder to feel safe. This could perpetuate a persistent state of fight or flight, which leads to a vicious cycle of anxiety.

This is why it's often difficult for people with CPTSD to develop healthy, long-lasting relationships. There might be little or no record of actually having nurturing and safe folks in your life for starters. Next, it's more difficult to perceive men and women as safe and nurturing even when they're.

Nevertheless, research shows us that attentional control can reduce attentional threat bias (Orcutt and Bardeen, 2011). This simply means that as you focus your attention on cues that allow you to be aware that you're safe, you now can find out to override the drive to focus on threats. Naturally, this only works if indeed you're in a safe scenario now. Practicing attentional control helps you be a much better detective and eliminate false positives in what you perceive as a threat in a situation or perhaps a safe person. As you start to be much better at understanding the safety cues in your environment, you begin to inhibit unnecessary defensive activation in mind and body.

The Takeaway

Healing from CPTSD involves recognizing that there's one other way to live. You're not condemned to repeat the patterns of your past. You can use the polyvagal theory that will help you heal from CPTSD using the following crucial steps:

Self-compassion: Establish self-compassion for your signs. Recognize the physiological, somatic basis of signs and the reason why you can't simply believe your way out of your trauma reactions.

Develop Somatic Awareness: Learn to mindfully track changes that are subtle in your body sensations and heart rate. Determine your very own personal signs of stress. This can help you respond instantly before the stress begins to feel overwhelming or perhaps out of your power. We call this lingering in the window of tolerance.

Work on Attentional Control: Practice concentrating your attention on specific cues in your environment that reminds you that you're safe now. Browse your area. Notice the light filtering through a window, an art piece on the wall, or perhaps how it feels to be reading this book. You can also listen to a popular piece of music, hold an item in your hand, or perhaps notice the calming fragrance of essential oil.

Remember, you're myelinating your social nervous system's neural pathways each time you feel secure, hooked up to a different person, or perhaps compassionate toward yourself. Every time you practice strengthening your social nervous system, it is going to become stronger. You can alter your physiology one day at the same time. Over time, it will become simpler to connect to positive states and override defensive symptoms associated with post-traumatic stress.

Chapter 5

Vagus Nerve Dysfunctions

Vagus Nerve Damage

Vagus nerve damage leads to several different symptoms, as this is much nerve that branches off to different areas of the body. The word' vagus' means wandering in Latin, and this name gives us an indication of the nerve's many pathways.

Damage to the vagus nerve's cranial nerve could be brought on by brain trauma, infection (encephalitis), the aging process, or perhaps chronic inflammation. The vagus nerve's primary role within the mind is usually to provide sensory innervation to the epidermis of the rear of the outer ear and the membranes of the ear canal. Hearing disorders, including tinnitus, aren't caused by CN X but appear to improve once the nerve is stimulated. Dental procedures and sinus infections can produce ear pain as they lie near the vagus nerve.

Referred pain from, for instance, late-stage throat cancer could also result in pain in the ear region due to nerve damage further down the line. Tick-Borne encephalitis and Lyme neuroborreliosis are both caused by tick bites; a tick bite can result in chronic or acute forms of brain infection in a tiny proportion of victims and attack the peripheral like the cranial nerves.

The nerve component that passes through the neck may be harmed by trauma, for instance, during surgery. It's very exposed as it runs alongside the internal jugular vein and carotid artery before splitting into a right and left pathway just above the aortic arch. Between its exit from the skull and this right and left splitting of ways, the vagus nerve plays both sensory and motor roles in the neck region.

Damage in and around the neck can result in a reduced gag reflex, loss or perhaps hoarseness of voice, trouble with speech and articulation, impaired swallowing, and - as mentioned previously - ear pain, if CN X is affected.

Vagus nerve trauma may additionally be the consequence of long term inflammatory, chronic, and autoimmune processes. These processes usually affect longer sections with increased symptoms like reduced gastric acid production, abnormal heart rate, blood pressure values, vomiting and nausea, abdominal pain, and slow gastric emptying (gastroparesis).

Vagus Nerve Disorders

Vagus nerve disorders are generally the outcome of disease or lesions and far less commonly a disorder solely of the vagus nerve. Tests for vagal damage range from evaluating the swallowing reflex to looking at stomach emptying using computed tomography - a CT scan. An endocrinologist may look a lot more carefully at glandular dysfunction associated with vagus nerve damage. Also, an ear-nose-throat doctor may wish to check for tumors and infections.

Nerve diseases can be autoimmune or hereditary. Nerves also degenerate over time, particularly in conjunction with poor nutrition and toxic lifestyle habits, including smoking and drinking too much alcohol. Like the other parts of the body, a lack of blood supply can harm one of the cranial nerves. Metabolic disorders like autoimmune diseases and diabetes-like multiple sclerosis can also be associated with vagus nerve disorders; even bacteria and viruses can attack nerve tissue. It's been already suggested that viral infections of the tenth cranial nerve might be in charge of disorders like chronic fatigue syndrome, post-traumatic stress disorder, and attention deficit hyperactivity disorder; however, several theories can be found all over the Internet, and evidence points to there being no singular cause.

Symptoms of Vagus Nerve Dysfunction

Very few folks understand what the vagus nerve is, , first and foremost, let me clarify that. The vagus nerve is probably the longest cranial nerve in the body regulating the gut and affects the cardiovascular, immune, endocrine, and respiratory systems. This means it is quite a major nerve in the human body. So when that nerve is dysfunctional, you can imagine it can have some very ridiculous side effects.

This past autumn, I worked out that my vagus nerve is, somehow, dysfunctional. And it turns out that a large number of individuals have a dysfunctional vagus nerve. When you have difficulty with vagus nerve dysfunction, you can be completely good for a while, catch a cold, or perhaps hit a wall, after which your body will take months to recover. I got very ill. I did not possess the power to actually get out of bed for days and likely would've withered away if my mother did not bring me food.

Living with vagus nerve dysfunction is something that you to live with because there's no cure. So in case you have a buddy with a dysfunction of the vagus nerve, please try and understand them and read through these common symptoms that accompany it.

1. Chronic nausea

Regrettably, this implies there is not a great deal that seems delicious to eat.

2. Weight loss

Thanks to not wanting to eat from nausea, you can lose considerable weight. At my worst, I unintentionally lost fifteen pounds in approximately three weeks.

3. Weight gain

Most likely because of chronic fatigue, anxiety, and depression.

4. Tachycardia and Bradycardia

Otherwise known as reduced heart rate and increased heart rate, respectfully. This could make easy things, like walking or possibly standing for extended periods, difficult.

5. IBS

Constant stomach pains and nausea generally means constantly feeling uncomfortable.

6. Depression

It is not merely because it is hooked up to your brain, but always feeling down and sick takes a toll on psychological health.

7. Anxiety

I still occasionally get panic attacks at the idea of leaving the house since I can have a terrible dizzy spell in public once again.

8. Chronic inflammation

It simply sucks.

9. Chronic fatigue

There is a difference between feeling exhausted all of the time since you are a college pupil and feeling tired since you are sick.

10. Heartburn

There is a difference between feeling exhausted all of the time since you are a college pupil and feeling tired since you are sick.
It does not matter exactly how in (or out) of shape you are.

11. Dizziness/fainting

We try our best to not stand up way too quickly because that'll help make it worse.

While there is no cure for vagus nerve dysfunction, there are many things we can do to control it. Several of us currently take medications for our psychological health and nausea. Yoga is always ideal for increasing muscle function. An enormous intake of salt and water is vital (we also consume a great deal of Gatorade). But it does not mean that we do not have bad days.

So try your very best to be there for your friends with dysfunctional vagus nerves. Rather than constantly suggesting to go out, maybe just ask if you can bring over many salty snacks and Gatorade and binge Netflix. It is going to be greatly appreciated.

Chapter 6

The Vagus Nerve and the Digestive System

Gastroparesis

Gastroparesis is a disorder that impacts the regular spontaneous movement of the muscles (motility) in your stomach. Typically, strong muscular contractions propel food through your intestinal tract. But if you have gastroparesis, your stomach's motility is slowed down or perhaps does not work at all, preventing your stomach from emptying properly.

The leading cause of gastroparesis is generally unfamiliar. At times it is a complication of diabetes, and some folks develop gastroparesis after surgery. Specific medications, such as opioid pain relievers, some antidepressants, and hypertension and allergy medications, can lead to slow gastric emptying and similar symptoms. For individuals who currently have gastroparesis, these prescription drugs could help make their condition worse.

Gastroparesis can interfere with normal digestion, abdominal pain, vomiting, and cause nausea. It can also cause issues with blood sugar levels and nutrition. Even though there is no cure for gastroparesis, changes to your diet, along with medication, can provide some relief.

Symptoms and signs of gastroparesis include:

- Abdominal pain
- Vomiting
- Nausea
- Abdominal bloating
- I am feeling bloated or full after eating just a few bites.
- Vomiting undigested food is eaten several hours earlier.
- Acid reflux
- Changes in blood sugar levels
- Lack of appetite
- Malnutrition and weight loss

Lots of people with gastroparesis do not have any apparent symptoms and signs.

Causes
It is never crystal clear what leads to gastroparesis, but in several instances, it could be brought on by damage to a nerve that controls the stomach muscles (vagus nerve).

The vagus nerve helps manage the complex tasks in your digestive system, including signaling your stomach muscles to contract and push food into the small intestine. A damaged vagus nerve cannot send signals usually to your stomach muscles. This might result in food to stay in your stomach a bit longer instead of moving into your small intestine to be digested.

Diseases can damage the vagus nerve and its branches, for example, diabetes, or even by surgery to the small intestine or the stomach.

Risk factors
Factors which can improve your risk of gastroparesis:

- Diabetes
- Esophageal or abdominal surgery

- Infection, typically from a virus
- Specific medications that slow the rate of stomach emptying, for example, narcotic pain medications
- Scleroderma - a connective tissue disease
- Nervous system diseases, like Parkinson's multiple sclerosis or disease
- Underactive thyroid (hypothyroidism) Women tend to be more prone to develop gastroparesis than are males.

Complications

Gastroparesis can cause several complications, such as:

- Severe dehydration. Ongoing vomiting can cause dehydration.
- Malnutrition. A feeble appetite can mean you do not take in enough calories or cannot absorb enough nutrients because of vomiting.
- Undigested food that hardens and stays in your stomach. Undigested food in your tummy can solidify into an excellent mass called a bezoar. Bezoars can cause vomiting and nausea and may be life-threatening if they prevent food from passing into your small intestine.
- Unpredictable blood sugar changes. Although gastroparesis does not result in diabetes, regular changes in the speed and amount of food passing into the small bowel can lead to erratic blood sugar levels. These variations in blood sugar make diabetes worse. In turn, lousy control of blood sugar levels makes gastroparesis even worse.
- Reduced quality of life. Signs can assist, make it challenging to get the job done and keep up with various other duties.

How Does The Vagus Nerve Support Every Aspect Of Digestion?

Your digestive system is dependent upon the Vagus Nerve for proper function. Most every aspect of regular digestion, motility (movement of the food/stool), and nutrient absorption depends upon adequate vagus nerve function. Without having the vagus nerve functioning, stool, and food doesn't adequately pass through the intestines normally.

The vagus nerve manages numerous aspects of ideal health! Let us take a look at some organs under the control of the vagus nerve.

Gallbladder:

The gallbladder stores bile, which, when launched, helps in the appropriate digestion of fats. The gallbladder function is under the command of the vagus nerve (both indirectly and direct).

Pancreas:

The pancreas produces pancreatic enzymes that assist in the absorption and digestion of nutrients, especially proteins and fats. The pancreas is partly controlled by the parasympathetic fibers originating in the dorsal vagal nucleus and the brain's ambiguous nucleus, now transported by the vagus nerve.

Sphincter of Oddi:

The vagus nerve activates the sphincter of Oddi to open, permitting digestive enzymes (from the pancreas) and bile (from the gallbladder) to pass into the intestines.

Intestines:

The vagus nerve triggers the intestines to push food (or chime) along the digestive system (peristalsis). Proper peristalsis moves the chime and blends, enabling correct nutrient absorption. Poor peristalsis can lead to gastroparesis, irregularity, bloating, and pain. The body absorbs free radicals and damaging contaminants if partially absorbed food sits in the intestinal tracts without moving. The effect may be chronic inflammation of the intestinal tract, leading to low nutrient absorption, pain or discomfort, and constipation (often alternating with diarrhea).

Inflammation:

Inflammation of the gut can bring about low motility (and diarrhea). The vagus nerve is crucial in controlling inflammation, both through its innervation with the spleen and its direct control of numerous inflammatory cells. The inflammatory cell's site under the vagus nerve's control is known as the alpha seven subunit nicotinic acetylcholine receptor (7nAChR). As the cholinergic anti-inflammatory pathway, it's dependent upon proper vagus nerve functioning.

The Brain-Gut Connection

If you have previously gone with your gut to create a decision or perhaps felt butterflies in your stomach when anxious, you are likely getting signals from a surprising source: your second brain. Hidden in the digestive system walls, this brain in your gut is revolutionizing medicine's understanding of the links between digestion, mood, health, and the way you think.

Researchers call this little brain the enteric nervous system (ENS). And it is not small. The ENS is two thin layers of over a hundred million nerve cells lining your gastrointestinal tract from the esophagus to rectum.

What Does Your Gut's Brain Manage?

Not like the big brain in your skull, the ENS cannot balance your checkbook or perhaps compose a love note. Its primary role is controlling digestion, from swallowing to the release of enzymes that break down food to control blood flow that can help with nutrient absorption to elimination. The enteric nervous system does not seem capable of thought as we understand it, but it communicates forth and back with our big brain - with powerful results.

The ENS may activate significant emotional shifts experienced by individuals coping with irritable bowel syndrome (Functional bowel and IBS) problems, including upset stomach., pain, bloating, diarrhea, and constipation. For decades, researchers and doctors believed that anxiety and depression contributed to these issues. But our studies and others indicate that it might also function as the other way around. Scientists find evidence that irritation in the gastrointestinal system may send signals to the central nervous system (CNS) that trigger mood changes.

These new findings might explain why a higher-than-normal percentage of individuals with functional bowel problems and IBS develop anxiety and depression. That is crucial because up to thirty to forty per cent of the population has functional bowel issues at some point.

New Gut Understanding Equals New Treatment Opportunities
This new understanding of the ENS CNS connection helps clarify the effectiveness of IBS and bowel disorder treatments like antidepressants and mind-body therapies as cognitive behavioral therapy (medical hypnotherapy and CBT). Our two brains talk' to one another, so therapies that help one may help another. In a way, gastroenterologists (medical professionals concentrating on gastrointestinal conditions) are like therapists searching for methods to alleviate the second brain.

Gastroenterologists may advise certain antidepressants for IBS, for instance - not since they believe the trouble is all in a patient's head, but because these medications calm symptoms in some cases by acting on nerve cells in the gut.

Psychological interventions as CBT can also help improve communications between the big brain and the brain in our gut, he says.

The vagus nerve and the neurological system neurons are cells found in your brain and the central nervous system that tell your body just how to behave. There are about a hundred billion neurons in the human brain.

Surprisingly, your gut contains 500 million neurons linked to your brain through nerves in your nervous system.

The vagus nerve is among probably the biggest nerves connecting your brain and gut. It sends signals in both directions.

For instance, in animal studies, stress inhibits the vagus nerve signals and leads to gastrointestinal problems.

Likewise, one study in humans found that individuals with irritable bowel syndrome (IBS) or perhaps Crohn's disease had reduced vagal tone, indicating a reduced function of the vagus nerve.

Interestingly, it was found that feeding mice a probiotic reduced the stress hormone level in their blood. Nevertheless, when their vagus nerve was cut, the probiotic did not affect them.

This implies that the vagus nerve is essential in the gut-brain axis and its role in stress.

Neurotransmitters

Your gut and brain can likewise be hooked up through chemicals called neurotransmitters.

Neurotransmitters produced in the brain control sensations and feelings.

For instance, the neurotransmitter serotonin contributes to feelings of happiness and helps control your body clock.

Surprisingly, many of these neurotransmitters can also be produced by your gut cells and the trillions of microbes living there. A huge proportion of serotonin is produced in the gut.

Your gut microorganisms likewise produce a neurotransmitter called gamma-aminobutyric acid (GABA), which helps control feelings of stress and anxiety, and fear.

Studies in laboratory mice have found that certain probiotics can up GABA production and reduce anxiety and depression-like behavior.

Gut Microbes Create Other Chemicals That Affect the Brain

The trillions of microorganisms that reside in your gut likewise make other chemicals that impact the way your mind works.

Your gut microorganisms produce great deals of short-chain fats (SCFA), for example, butyrate, acetate, and propionate.

They make SCFA by digesting fiber. SCFA affects brain function in a variety of ways, like reducing appetite.

One study discovered that consuming propionate can reduce food intake and lessen the brain's activity associated with reward from high energy food.

The microbes, butyrate, and another SCFA that make it can also be crucial for forming the blood and the brain's barrier, known as the blood-brain barrier.

Gut microorganisms also metabolize bile acids and amino acids to produce numerous other chemical substances that affect the brain.

Bile acids are chemicals generated by the liver that are generally associated with taking in dietary fats. They may also affect the brain.

Two studies in mice found that social disorders and anxiety reduce bile acids' production by gut bacteria and alter the genes involved in their production.

Gut Microbes Affect Inflammation
Your gut-brain axis is hooked up through the immune system.

Gut and gut microbes play a crucial part in your immune system and inflammation by controlling what's passed into the body and what's excreted.

If your immune system is turned on for very long, it can lead to inflammation related to different brain disorders like anxiety and Alzheimer's illness.

Lipopolysaccharide (LPS) is an inflammatory contaminant made by some germs. If a lot of it passes from the gut into the blood, it can result in inflammation.

This may happen as soon as the gut barrier becomes leaky, enabling LPS and bacteria to cross over into the blood.

Inflammation and high LPS in the blood have been related to various brain disorders such as severe depression, schizophrenia, and dementia.

Prebiotics, Probiotics, and the Gut-Brain Axis

Gut bacteria affect brain health, so altering your gut bacteria may enhance your brain health.

Probiotics are living bacteria that impart health benefits if eaten. Nevertheless, not all probiotics are the same.

Probiotics that affect the brain are known as psychobiotics.

Some probiotics have been proven to improve stress, depression, and anxiety.

One little study of individuals with irritable bowel syndrome and mild-to-moderate anxiety or perhaps depression found that taking a probiotic Bifidobacterium long NCC3001 for six weeks significantly improved symptoms.

Prebiotics, which are fibers that are fermented by your gut bacteria, may also affect brain health.

One study discovered that taking a prebiotic called galactooligosaccharides for three weeks significantly reduced the level of stress hormone in the body called cortisol.

Conclusion

The gut-brain axis describes the chemical and physical connections between your brain and gut.

Millions of neurons and nerves run between your brain and gut. Other chemical compounds and neurotransmitters produced in your gut likewise impact your mind.

By modifying the types of germs in your gut, it can be simple to improve your brain health.

Omega-3 essential fatty acids, fermented foods, probiotics, along with other polyphenol-rich foods, may help your gut health, which could benefit the gut-brain axis.

Chapter 7

Immune Activation and Inflammation

Inflammation is generally a temporary and local event and, upon its physiological, immune, and resolution, homeostasis is restored. Nevertheless, disrupted innate immune regulation can result in continual pro-inflammatory cytokine activity and chronic or excessive inflammation. This state underlies a range of disease syndromes' pathogenesis, rheumatoid arthritis, including sepsis, inflammatory bowel disease, and other inflammatory and autoimmune disorders. Understanding endogenous mechanisms that prevent or perhaps neutralize excessive pro-inflammatory responses could lead to novel healing options for diseases linked to an extreme or chronic inflammatory state.

Chronic inflammation as an outcome of metabolic and immune dysregulation is a distinctive feature in patients with obesity. It is causally related to insulin resistance and other metabolic complications. Reduced vagus nerve activity in the context of being obese has been reported. Selective cholinergic activation within the efferent vagus nerve mediated arm of the inflammatory reflex can suppress obesity-associated inflammation and reverse metabolic complications. These results raise the interesting possibility that dysregulation of vagus nerve mediated signaling might contribute to the pathogenesis of obesity and its related comorbidities.

In this review, we present a conceptual view of the inflammatory reflex as a biological mechanism that functions on the path between metabolism and immunity and could be exploited to treat obesity-associated inflammation and obesity-related disorders.

The inflammatory reflex

Communication between the immune system, in addition to the mind, is necessary for managing inflammation. The inflammatory reflex is a centrally integrated physiological mechanism in which afferent vagus nerve signaling, activated by pathogen-derived items or cytokines, is functionally connected with efferent Vagus Nerve mediated output to manage pro-inflammatory cytokine production and swelling. The lack of this inflammatory reflex - resulting from genetic ablation or neural lesions of essential components - leads to excessive innate immune responses and cytokine toxicity. The inflammatory reflex has been reviewed elsewhere.

Afferent arm

Afferent vagus nerve fibers sense peripheral inflammatory molecules and convey signals to the mind and are essential for immune-to-brain communication. Afferent vagus neurons, residing in the nodose and jugular ganglia, terminate primarily in the nucleus tractus solitarius in the brainstem medulla oblongata. Afferent signaling is even more communicated through neural contacts between brainstem nuclei, the hypothalamus, and forebrain regions related to the integration of visceral sensory info and coordination of behavioral responses and autonomic function.

Peripheral administration of bacterial lipopolysaccharide (also known as endotoxin) or IL-1β causes afferent vagus nerve activation, as determined by increased c-Fos expression and electrical activity. IL-1β receptors expressed on vagus nerve afferents and chemosensory (glomus) cells in paraganglia surrounding afferent vagus nerve endings have been implicated in recognizing immune activation. Prostaglandin-dependent mechanisms have also been implicated in activating vagus nerve afferents by increasing levels of circulating IL-1β. Intraportal administration of IL-1β to rats increases afferent and, subsequently, efferent vagus nerve and splenic nerve activity. Peripheral immune stimulation causes sickness behavior, attenuated in rodents who have undergone surgical transection of the vagus nerve to prevent immune signaling at peripheral nerve endings. This attenuation is dependent on the magnitude of immune activation because fairly large quantities of circulating IL-1β produce fever and sickness behavior by bypassing the neural circuits, acting through brain circumventricular organs (including the area postrema), and via other humoral mechanisms. Accordingly, afferent vagus nerve endings appear to be important for relaying information about immune status to the brain when proinflamma tory cytokines are present at fairly low levels. Nevertheless, TLR4 (which can be activated by lipopolysaccharide) is conveyed in the nodose ganglion, suggesting a mechanism by which lipopolysaccharide and other inflammatory molecules can activate vagus nerve afferents above their visceral endings.

Efferent arm

A little more than a decade ago, an important role of efferent vagus nerve cholinergic signaling in brain-to-immune communication was revealed by observations that vagus nerve stimulation suppresses local and serum pro-inflammatory cytokine levels in rodents with endo-toxemia. That acetylcholine inhibits the release of TNF, IL-1β, and IL-18 from lipopolysaccharide-stimulated macrophages. These outcomes led to the definition of the cholinergic anti-inflammatory pathway as the efferent vagus nerve based arm of the inflammatory reflex. This efferent arm can be centrally regulated, and muscarinic acetylcholine receptors in the brain have been implicated in this regulation. Galantamine is a centrally acting acetylcholinesterase inhibitor and activates the efferent cholinergic arm of the inflammatory reflex through a muscarinic receptor-dependent mechanism in the human brain. Defining a brain network that may be used to explore central mechanisms of inflammatory reflex control is the aim of ongoing studies.

In peripheral tissues, the α7 nicotinic acetylcholine receptor (α7nAChR) is vital for mediating anti-inflammatory signaling within the efferent arm of the inflammatory reflex. Accordingly, several α7nAChR agonists have been identified as experimental anti-inflammatory therapeutics with the potential for clinical development. The α7 subunit of the receptor is expressed in macrophages, monocytes, dendritic cells, T cells, endothelial and other non-neuronal cells, and the functional and structural characterization of non-neuronal α7nAChRs is an area of study that is constant. The presence of α7nAChRs on bone marrow-derived cells is necessary for the inflammatory reflex's functional integrity, but their presence on neuronal cells and cells isn't vital. The anti-inflammatory action of α7nAChR agonists or vagus nerve stimulation is associated with the downregulation of TLR4 and CD14 expression in immune cells. Cholinergic inhibition of pro-inflammatory cytokine production is mediated through intracellular signal pathways downstream of α7nAChR that culminate in suppressing NF-κB nuclear translocation. The tyrosine-protein kinase JAK2 might also be recruited as well as activated by α7nAChR upon cholinergic stimulation. Subsequent phosphorylation of the transcription factor STAT3 results in suppression of pro-inflammatory cytokine production in intestinal macrophages.

The anti-inflammatory results of vagus nerve stimulation in animals with endotoxemia require neural signals along the splenic adrenergic nerve, which comes from the celiac ganglion innervated by the efferent vagus nerve. Somewhat by chance, a certain subset of T cells (memory CD4+ T cells, which express adrenoreceptors), rather than neurons, provide an endogenous source of acetylcholine in the spleen. T cell production of acetylcholine in the spleen is vital for the inflammatory reflex. In nude mice, which lack T cells, Vagus Nerve stimulation fails to suppress TNF levels during endotoxemia. Nevertheless, the transfer of acetylcholine producing T cells, which repopulate the spleen in nude mice, restores the neural circuit's integrity.

Along with this spleen mediated mechanism in endotoxemia, efferent vagus nerve endings might directly regulate the immune function by releasing acetylcholine, without the requirement for either signaling along the splenic nerve or perhaps T cells. Such an immediate mechanism has been implicated in suppressing inflammation in experimental settings of hemorrhagic shock, ileus, inflammatory bowel disease, autoimmune myocarditis, and other inflammatory and autoimmune conditions. Importantly, a lot of these conditions are associated with autonomic dysfunction and decreased vagus nerve tone. Enhancement of vagus nerve output could, thus, have healing potential in these settings.

Vagus Nerve in metabolic regulation

Efferent signaling and vagus nerve afferents have a crucial role in regulating feeding behavior and metabolic homeostasis. This finely tuned regulation aims to preserve preventing fluctuations and energy balance in metabolism and body weight, which may be detrimental to the individual.

Nutritional intake and metabolism

Vagus nerve afferents innervating the gastrointestinal tract and liver are major constituents of a sensory system that spot modifications in metabolic molecules and micronutrients. These nerve fibers transmit info detected by associated mechanoreceptors, specific metabolite receptors, and chemoreceptors in the gut and hepatic portal system concerning levels of lipids, peptide YY, leptin, cholecystokinin, glucose, and insulin on the human brain. Vagus nerve efferents, on the other hand, supply brain-derived output to the gastrointestinal system, pancreas, and liver. Vagus nerve innervation of white adipose tissue has been demonstrated using retrograde neuronal tracing. Nonetheless, some other researchers found limited retrograde labeling in the dorsal motor nucleus following the injection of the tracer into white adipose tissue along with a lack of some parasympathetic markers in adipose tissue. Thus, anatomy, along with the vagus nerve's practical role in adipose tissue, is an effective study area.

Gastrointestinal and hepatic vagus nerve afferents are associated with the regulation of short-term feeding behavior. Afferent vagus nerve signaling mediates gastric cholecystokinin induced satiety and meal termination. Synergistic activation of vagus nerve afferents by cholecystokinin and leptin mediates their short-term inhibitory effects on food intake. Lipid accumulation on top of the intestine, and consequent intestinal cholecystokinin release, also triggers vagus brain-integrated and nerve-mediated suppressive hepatic glucose production. Furthermore, this reflex mechanism's efferent arm can easily be activated by direct activation of neurons in the dorsal vagal complex.

Glucose-induced pancreatic insulin secretion can be stimulated by treatment with a truncated form of glucagon-like peptide 1, which activates hepatic vagus nerve afferents and, subsequently, vagus nerve afferents innervating the pancreas. Along with its intrinsic effects on the enteric nervous system, glucose in the lumen of the gastrointestinal tract causes neuronal activation in vagus nerve afferents, the nucleus tractus solitarius, the arcuate hypothalamic nucleus as well as the dorsal motor nucleus, thus highlighting the role of the brain circuitry in vagus nerve regulation of pancreatic secretion and gastrointestinal function.

Additionally, metabolic molecules can act right in the brain to trigger efferent output that regulates metabolic homeostasis. Insulin signaling in the mediobasal hypothalamus is mediated through modulation of ATP-sensitive potassium channels and has been implicated in suppressing hepatic glucose production. Efferent vagus nerve signaling to the liver is crucial for this particular regulation. Hypothalamic sensing of fluctuations in circulatory lipid levels triggers efferent vagus nerve mediated output regulating hepatic glucose production and glucose homeostasis. In the hypothalamus, cholinergic activation dependent on muscarinic receptors increases hepatic glycogen synthesis through a mechanism mediated by the vagus nerve. Vagus nerve derived cholinergic signaling through a mechanism mediated by M3 muscarinic receptors has been implicated in stimulating insulin release in the pancreas.

The dorsal vagal complex and different hypothalamic regions are important constituents of a brain network associated with vagus nerve mediated regulation of peripheral metabolic functions. Interconnections between these and other forebrain regions have a job in integrating efferent and afferent signaling in terms of the control of the regulation and metabolic homeostasis of motivational and hedonic factors of feeding behavior.

Postprandial inflammation

Serum lipopolysaccharide levels in healthy individuals are increased after consuming a high fat, or perhaps high-carbohydrate and high-fat meals. Endotoxaemia following high-fat diet ingestion or perhaps lipid intake has been implicated in postprandial inflammation as plasma levels of IL 6 and also the expression of TLR4, SOCS3, and TLR2 in mononuclear cells increases. Postprandial endotoxemia and inflammation are transient, nonetheless, and information from some studies suggests that the vagus nerve, as well as the inflammatory reflex, might have a role in suppressing postprandial inflammation. Afferent vagus nerve signaling has the main role in telling the brain about peripheral inflammation during exposure to low levels of pro-inflammatory stimuli. TLR4, which is conveyed by vagus nerve afferents, provides a molecular sensory component for neural detection of lipopolysaccharide in postprandial inflammation.

Dietary lipid infusion causes cholecystokinin release, which acts both via vagus nerve afferents and straight in the brain to trigger activation of efferent vagus nerve signaling, which subsequently suppresses the release of pro-inflammatory cytokines. IL-1β potentiates activation of vagus nerve afferents by cholecystokinin or leptin. Moreover, in rats, truncal vagotomy is associated with increased bacterial translocation across the intestinal mucosa, suggesting a tonic vagus nerve control of intestinal permeability and postprandial endotoxemia.

The inflammatory reflex and obesity

Disruption in immune and metabolic homeostasis in obesity is associated with hyperglycemia, insulin resistance, hypertension, and dyslipidemia. This particular group of conditions characterizes metabolic syndrome. Furthermore, acute-phase proteins and pro-inflammatory cytokines like CRP are increased in people with obesity, indicating chronic inflammation. This inflammatory state is regarded as a crucial pathophysiological constituent in obesity, underlying its negative consequences and linking it to other metabolic syndrome parts. Many lines of evidence suggest that vagus nerve activity can be impaired in obesity, and enhancing cholinergic signaling within the inflammatory reflex can suppress obesity-associated inflammation and its negative implications.

Inflammation and obesity pathogenesis

The characteristic inflammatory state in obesity has been thoroughly discussed elsewhere. White adipose tissue in individuals with obesity is expanded and infiltrated with T cells, bone-marrow-derived macrophages, mast cells, and B cells. As a result, this tissue becomes a significant source of pro-inflammatory factors. Adipocyte enlargement resulting from increased lipid deposition leads to metabolic alterations associated with dysregulated secretion of adipokines, resistin, including leptin, visfatin, and adiponectin. Furthermore, hypoxia and cell death occur in adipose tissue, leading to increased macrophage recruitment and generation of reactive oxygen species, which promote inflammation. Increased release and production of TNF, IL 6, CCL2, and other pro-inflammatory mediators from adipocytes and activated M1 macrophages and other immune cells also drive inflammation. Along with fatty tissue, activation of inflammatory pathways also occurs in the liver, skeletal muscle, and brain.

Adipocyte and macrophage expression of TLR4 and TLR2 provides a mechanism for transforming metabolic overload (high levels of saturated free fatty acids and glucose) into pro-inflammatory responses, such as free fatty acids glucose can be ligands for TLRs. Subsequent intracellular signaling mediated through JNK, IKK, and PKR leads to stimulation of the transcription factors NF-κB and AP-1 and increased pro-inflammatory mediators production. Metabolic overload also results in endoplasmic reticulum stress associated with JNK and IKK signaling and generation of reactive oxygen species, triggering inflammation. Additionally, activation of macrophages and T cells in the adipose tissue of patients with obesity may be mediated by inflammasomes. As occurs in individuals with type two diabetes mellitus, Pancreatic islet inflammation can likewise be mediated by these protein complexes.

The intestinal microflora also contributes to the development of inflammation in people with obesity. Chronic ingestion of a high-fat diet plan increases the proportion of lipopolysaccharides containing microbiota in this increase. The gut is associated with low-grade metabolic endotoxemia in both humans and mice. In mice, mimicking metabolic endotoxemia by chronic administration of a low dose of lipopolysaccharide results in inflammation, increased adiposity, metabolic complications, and weight gain. These changes result from the activation of CD14 TLR4 signaling, which triggers the increased production of pro-inflammatory cytokines by macrophages and adipocytes.

The role of certain cytokines and adipokines in mediating obesity-associated complications has been the subject of numerous reviews. Inflammation is causally linked with impaired insulin signaling in peripheral target tissues and insulin resistance, a significant complication in obesity and type two diabetes mellitus. Activation of inflammatory pathways in the brain interferes with insulin and leptin signaling in the mind and contributes to insulin resistance. Increased lipolysis in insulin-resistant adipose tissue leads to enhanced release of free fats, stimulating inflammatory reactions, and reinforcing insulin resistance. Pro-inflammatory cytokines and adipokines can inhibit insulin signaling by targeting The insulin or IRS proteins receptor. Specifically, TNF induces inhibition of insulin activated tyrosine phosphorylation of the insulin receptor and serine phosphorylation of IRS 1, which leads to inactivation of insulin signaling. Other pro-inflammatory cytokines and TNF act in a paracrine manner to stimulate JNK, IKK, and most likely other kinases and mediate serine phosphorylation of IRS proteins. Additionally, pro-inflammatory cytokines such as TNF, IL 6, and adipokine resistin induce SOCS proteins' expression, which blocks insulin signaling through inhibition of insulin receptor tyrosine kinase activity or perhaps IRS 1 ubiquitination and degradation. The overall result is a bad influence of pro-inflammatory cytokines on insulin signaling.

Conclusions

The inflammatory reflex mediated by the vagus nerve continues to be effectively exploited therapeutically in preclinical models of diseases with aetiologies characterized by excessive inflammatory responses. Insufficient efferent vagus nerve cholinergic output might have a causative role in the dysfunctional immune and metabolic regulation observed in obesity, as selective activation of the efferent cholinergic arm of the inflammatory reflex attenuates both inflammation and metabolic derangements. Although cholinergic suppression of inflammation can contribute specifically to alleviating metabolic complications, direct cholinergic effects on metabolic pathways may also help alleviate symptoms associated with metabolic syndrome, and type two diabetes mellitus. These complex interactions and the contribution of peripheral and central mechanisms in this regulation are ongoing topics of study. Additionally, intracellular mechanisms by which cholinergic signals control obesity-associated inflammation and modulate insulin signaling are under investigation. The α7nAChR agonists, centrally acting acetylcholinesterase inhibitors, and direct electrical stimulation of the vagus nerve offer potential therapeutic strategies for dealing with obesity, metabolic syndrome, type two diabetes mellitus, and various other disorders associated with obesity. The use of cholinergic modalities, together with existing or perhaps new therapeutic approaches to target immune, endocrine, and neural functions for therapeutic benefit in patients with obesity-related disorders, should also be considered.

How is your reading going?

Hi there!

I hope you are enjoying the reading; do you find the information useful?

I've put all my experience and research into the book, I hope you are liking the book!

If you find the information are valuable and interesting, I'd like to kindly ask for your support by leaving a review on Amazon. It would only take 30 seconds of your time, but it would make a huge difference to me, and it would help other people like you finding some valuable insights on the topic they are interested in.

>>You can Leave a Review Here<<

https://swiy.io/VagusNerveReviewAMZ

Or Scan This Code With your Phone Camera

If you have any feedback, please get in touch with me at the following contacts, I have them at the beginning of the book, but for your convenience, I've dropped them here too!

Website: sharoncopeland.com

Email: info@sharoncopeland.com

Facebook Page: https://swiy.io/SharonCopelandFBPage

Facebook Support Book:
https://swiy.io/SharonCopelandFBGroup

Instagram: @saroncopelandauthor

Free Workbook

To help you take some "me" time and reflect on which actions to take after the reading, I have prepared a workbook with some key questions to ask yourself. I hope this helps!

You can find the workbook at the following link.

https://swiy.io/VagusNerveWorkbookLP

Or Scan This Code With your Phone Camera

Happy Reading!

Chapter 8

Overcome Stress with the Vagus Nerve

Emotional stress can influence your physical and mental health, so finding ways to handle it should be a high priority. You will find techniques to help manage stress, decrease pain, boost healing, and regulate our nervous system for a decreased stress response.

Have you ever heard of a flight or fight? When we experience sudden stress that is excessive, we activate our flight or fight response, getting the body prepared to flee the scene or fight. There's no place to run and hide in our daily stress experience, and the tense situation isn't one that can be easily fought off. Many of us aren't meeting tigers in the street!

During persistent high-stress situations, the body remains in high gear, with hormonal stress agents as adrenaline and cortisol flowing through the body. This develops wear and tear on the body and mind, and in time can produce a large range of health problems such as chronic pain, mood swings, anxiety, gut inflammation, and a lot more.

The best part is that our bodies contain their superpower to decrease our flight or fight response.

The vagus nerve system serves to counterbalance the fight or flight system and may also bring a relaxation response in our body. It's among the cranial nerves that connect the mind to the body. The vagus nerve is a significant component of how our bodies and brains function. Without it, our bodies would not do simple tasks. By activating it, we can receive powerful health benefits.

One of the primary ways you can stimulate the vagus nerve's healthy function is through deep, slow belly breathing. You can find out to use breathing exercises to shift your focus from pain or even stress. The human brain processes one thing at a time. In case you concentrate on the rhythm of your breath, you are not centered on the stressor.

The moment we expect stress in any form, nearly all of us are likely to stop breathing and hold our breath. Breath-holding activates the fight/flight/freeze response; it tends to boost the sensation of pain, anxiety, stiffness, and fear. To exercise deep breathing, inhale through your nose and exhale through your mouth; remember to:

- Breathe slower (aim for six breaths per minute).
- Breathe deeper, from the belly. Consider expanding your abdomen and widening your rib cage as you inhale.
- Exhale more than you inhale. It is the exhale that triggers the relaxation response.

Additional strategies for activating the vagus nerve include:

- Gargling with water or singing activates our vocal cords.
- Foot massage: a firm or gentle touch can help in stimulating the vagus nerve.
- Coldwater face immersion: immerse your forehead, eyes, and a minimum of 2/3 of both cheeks into the cool water. This generates the vagus nerve, decreases heart rate, promotes the intestinal tracts, and switches the body's immune system.

- Eating fiber promotes vagus impulses to the brain, slowing gut motions and making us feel fuller after meals.
- Laughter: having a great laugh lifts your state of mind, boosts your body's immune system, and likewise stimulates the vagus nerve.

We don't usually have to let stressful situations negatively affect our bodies and minds. We can activate our vagus nerve to send out a message to our bodies that it is time to unwind and de-stress, resulting in long-term improvements in mood, pain management, resilience, and well-being.

The Vagus Nerve being the Key to our Well-being.

Take a deep breath—hug from a pal. Grab the ceiling and stretch your limbs. All these fundamental acts bestow a sense of convenience and calm. And each works its calming magic in part by activating a complicated system of nerves that connects the mind to the heart, the gut, the immune system, and great deals of the organs. The product is known jointly as the vagus nerve.

The vagus nerve is amongst the 12 cranial nerves, sprawl out from the mind and into the body like a complicated network of roots. These nerve networks function as lines of communication between the body and the mind's great deals of organs and systems. Several of the cranial nerves analyze sensory info gathered by the skin, eyes, or possibly tongue. Others manage muscles or perhaps cooperate with glands.

While electronic stimulation holds assurance - and, in some situations, has already been providing relief - for individuals with a range of ailments, there are lots of ways to stimulate vagal activity without a device or perhaps implant. We understand that massage and yoga promote parasympathetic nervous system activity, which is a vagal activity.

Research indicates that these, as well as numerous related activities, increase vagal activity via pressure receptors buried beneath the surface area of your skin - receptors located throughout the body, and ones that only firm pressure or perhaps a full stretch can reach. It is highlighted that light stroking or touching is arousing, while a bear hug or powerful handshake is inherently soothing. A good hug or perhaps a handshake promote parasympathetic activity.

Just about anything that folks find relaxing - meditation, deep breathing - is associated with heightened vagal and parasympathetic nervous system activity. We did studies in history, showing that patients with migraine have impaired vagal activity. We attempted to resolve that by doing yoga or perhaps deep breathing meditation, and we found a lot of those things enabled us to trigger the vagal nerve. On the other hand, tension and stress, and anxiety are related to depressed vagal activity, describing why they are connected to an increased threat for various other disorders.

There is still a great deal about the vagus nerve science that we do not understand. But as doctors uncover much more of its secrets, these discoveries reveal new and more efficient methods to alleviate pain, sadness, inflammation, and disease.

The Role of the Vagus Nerve in Stress Management

Called the social engagement system, the ventral vagal network runs upward from the diaphragm location to the brain stem, crossing over nerves in the lungs, throat, neck, and eyes. Actions involving these areas of the body - including deep breaths, humming, gargling, or perhaps even social cues like smiling or making eye contact with someone - send messages to the brain that it is okay to relax.

Basic activities like taking a full breath and hugging your pet or even a friend, stretching your limbs and reaching for the ceiling, all these basic acts bestow a sense of comfort and calm. And each works its soothing magic by activating a complex system of nerves that connects the mind to the heart, the gut, the immune system, and lots of the organs. The product is known collectively as the vagus nerve.

Recently, research has uncovered brand new info, which has given us a much better appreciation of the vagus nerve's job in wellness and health, so let us a better look at some of this info.

The 10th cranial nerve or the vagus nerve is probably the longest, biggest, and most complex of the cranial nerves, and in many ways, it is also the least understood. Industry experts have linked its activity to symptom changes in people with migraine headaches, inflammatory bowel disease, arthritis, epilepsy, depression, and many other common problems.

The greater part of science learns about the vagus nerve, the more often it looks like a clear understanding of its function could unlock new doors to treating all manner of human suffering while helping us support our entire body in much better management of anxiety and stress.

Vagus is Latin for wandering, which is suitable when considering all the areas the vagus nerve reaches. It seems like every year, and it finds a new system or organ that it communicates with.

Branches of the vagus nerve are attached to the face and voice. We know that depressed individuals have low vagal activity related to much less intonation and less active facial expressions. A specific branch of the vagus nerve runs right down to the gastrointestinal tract. Below, low vagal activity is associated with slowed gastric motility, which interferes with proper digestion.

Still, various other vagus nerve branches are hooked up to the heart, the immune system, and the lungs. The vagus nerve's activation or perhaps deactivation is linked with the ebb or perhaps flow of hormones like cortisol and the intestinal hormone ghrelin, the amount of inflammation the immune system produces, and numerous other internal processes which shape human experience and health.

There is an enormous bioelectrical and biochemical series of events that the vagus nerve is accountable for, and all that's nearly impossible to map.

Exactly how could one nerve system control so much? While some vagal activity elements are inscrutable, it is apparent that this nerve is the governor of the parasympathetic nervous system, which will help control the body's relaxation responses.

In easy terms, heightened vagal activity counteracts the stress response, which involves the sympathetic nervous system. The sympathetic nervous system is flight or fight. In contrast, the parasympathetic nervous system is accountable for healing and repair.

Heightened vagal activity slows the heart rate and switches off inflammation, in part by triggering the release of immune system calming chemicals.

There is also evidence that activating the vagus nerve through electrical stimulation can produce various health benefits. We know that the stimulation frequency can turn off an asthma attack or perhaps an epileptic seizure. It can turn off a migraine or perhaps cluster headache, and yes, it can reduce the perception of acid reflux steadily.

Choose practically any common problem intensified by inflammation or stress - everything from arthritis to inflammatory bowel illness. The research study is showing that vagus nerve stimulation can assist treat or possibly ease symptoms. Additionally, it can improve the body's defense versus illness and viruses.

In the past, this stimulation required a surgical implant in the chest that transmits electrical pulses right into the vagus nerve. But some more recent, non-invasive devices are available that can treat migraine and cluster headaches and stimulate the vagus nerve when pressed against the neck's skin.

More and more, we're learning just how critical vagal activity is to mood and attention. There is currently proof that stimulating the vagus nerve may improve working memory or help individuals with attention deficit hyperactivity disorder. We are aware that stimulating the vagus nerve can help with the treatment of some types of depression.

The very best part is you will discover extremely easy things that you can do in your home to help stimulate the vagus nerve. Calming yourself allows you to think clearly and process your difficult situations - that will solve more stress. Here are a couple of simple strategies:

1. Tune into just how your body feels

If you are not alert to how your body feels when you are stressed, it is difficult to determine if you have to give your nervous system some relaxation. The first action is to rest and digest, focus on your body's sensations.

It is recommended to note your body's baseline physical state when you are calm, so you can notice how stress changes your entire body. Extend your legs, go for a stroll, or perhaps even bend over and touch your toes, noticing what feels good and what doesn't. The more we recognize our bodies' limitations and capabilities, the more often we can take proper care of them.

When you have a broad knowledge of your body's baseline, you can see the little ways stress impacts you physically. For instance, you may feel your shoulders slightly tense when you read through the news. Next, you can take some time to relax them - an act of compassionate self-care that not only relieves physical pain but signals to your ventral vagus nerve, you are in a safe place.

2. Monitor and regulate your breath

Conscious breathing, or perhaps paying attention that is focused on your breath, could be a powerful self-regulation method. Specifically, deep breathing directly activates the ventral vagal system because the Vagus Nerve travels through the vocal cables.

A study reveals that mindful, deep breathing from the diaphragm reduces cortisol, the stress hormone. In a 2017 study, individuals who participated in a guided breathing program lowered their cortisol (stress hormone) levels in their saliva immediately after the physical exercise.

Nevertheless, there's a recommended technique. The exhale is among the most critical aspects of mindful breathing. Exhaling more than you inhale puts the ventral vagal network into action and promotes the rest and digest response.

3. Compassionate attention

Whether with many other folks or perhaps through compassionate attention to yourself, social connection is among the most crucial methods to activate the ventral vagal network. You cannot go out with friends due to practicing social distancing. Even so, you can FaceTime a loved one or even have a meaningful discussion with someone you are isolating with. Establishing a sense of connection and safety with someone - and making eye contact, quite possibly over a Zoom meeting - can cue your body to relax.

When there is no one to get friendly with, or even if blurry, online interactions just are not cutting it; you can visualize someone you trust - even a pet - and imagine feelings of connection and safety. Or perhaps you can simply hunker down in a relaxing room in your house. If you are stuck in your house, looking for safety cues in your space or perhaps with another person can activate the ventral vagal system.

4. Harness anxious thoughts

The story you inform yourself about your stressors can determine the method your body responds.

The way you interpret your situation and its danger lays out the possibility of how chronic your stress will be. In case you know external stressors are not likely to change shortly, it is essential to minimize your perception of the threat by shifting the way you respond emotionally. Release the disappointment or perhaps pressure of what you can't change and allow yourself to concentrate more on solutions you do have control over. For example, instead of thinking about social distancing as being stuck in your home forever, think about being home as a means to help public health and an opportunity to slow down.

Steering your thoughts in a far more hopeful direction might result in the brain to send messages through the vagus nerve, triggering calm in all the organs and systems along the way.

One of the methods to do that is by using your five senses. Going outdoors, listening to birds, and smelling a flower are all simple grounding activities, which could help activate the ventral vagus nerve. These things bring your body to the current moment, which might feel more secure to your central nervous system than the possible scenarios of the future.

When you pay attention to both your body and head under stress, you will feel far more relaxed - and eventually, a lot more yourself. When you are in the hyped-up state of perceiving everything as a threat, all your resources will try to keep it together. In case you attempt to deal with your emotional response, you will have a lot more resources and power to problem solve.

Chapter 9

The Role of the Vagus Nerve in Social Engagements

My clients wonder why, in certain situations, they behave as calm, loving, enlightened people towards their partners, and also sometimes, they yell and scream at the person they love, surprising even themselves.

Or perhaps they can be socializing with folks they know very well, with plenty of confidence, eye contact, and good interpersonal exchange. But when someone they do not trust enters the group, they shut down, stumble over their words, and would like to hit out (usually verbally) or perhaps hide.
Neuroscientist Steven W. Porges Ph.D., director of the Brain-Body Centre at the Faculty of Illinois, Chicago, might have come up with an answer to these perplexing behavioral changes. He says that engaging socially, participating, and smiling in calm conversations is excellent for us. In his Polyvagal Theory of Emotion (1995), Dr. Porges proposes that when we enhance our connection with many other folks, we trigger neural circuits in our bodies that calm the heart, relax the gut, and switch off the fear effect.

The vagus nerve is central to Dr. Porges' theory. It's a sophisticated pathway that carries messages quickly from the brain stem to the heart, intestines, and lungs. It regulates some facial muscles, like the ear, can improve our ability to give others appropriate facial cues and better listen to them.

The vagus nerve affects our heart rate and breathing and is needed in just how we perceive, react to, and recover from stress. When the vagus nerve is activated, we work through a system that Dr. Porges calls the social engagement system.

For instance, under social conditions where we feel confident, our heart rate and breathing slow down, our blood pressure drops, and our stress response turns off. Our bodies launch into a state of physical calm. We are secure enough to move closer to a different person, making intimacy possible.

Thus, social engagement enhances our sense of safety, creating a good feedback loop that leads to more calming. But there is a catch. We need to feel safe to enter the body, and this particular condition unconsciously decides when we're safe and when we're not. If the body detects that we're in "danger," it changes to the fight/flight response, driven by the body's HPA (hypothalamic-pituitary-adrenal) axis translates into symptoms of anxiety in the contemporary world.

Dr. Porges says that our stress response is organized hierarchically through the autonomic nervous system. The public communication neural circuits, involving facial expression, listening and speech, inhibit more primitive (reptilian) systems, like mobilization (fight/flight behaviors) and immobilization (feigning death, fainting).

Evolution has created this three-tiered system of "wiring," which used to be adaptive and helped us to respond to immediate danger.

Tier 1

When we are safe, we're generally operating through the social engagement system, via the myelinated vagus nerve, which is probably the most advanced of our evolutionary responses. It supports our capacity to engage socially with others, connecting the cranial nerves related to the face, voice, and ears with the heart, lungs, and gut. It improves our ability to create appropriate facial cues, like smiling and improving our hearing and verbal fluency. Messages back and forth from the brain travel faster when we're in a state of social engagement.

Tier 2

When we feel in danger, the fight/flight response is mobilized, and at this time, we typically find it impossible to work through the social engagement system. The fight or flight response functions through the more primitive, sympathetic branch of the autonomic nervous system - the HPA axis - which leads to rage and/or fear in humans.

Activation of the sympathetic pathway is the biological equivalent of pushing a panic button, and also we revert to this pattern when we're under too much stress. This describes why we can suddenly lose our social beauty. Our increased stimulation leads us to be tongue-tied, clumsy, and tense when somebody we might not rely on enters the room. Even the muscles in our ears tighten up so that our hearing is compromised. We might encounter internal organ dysfunction, such as gastrointestinal issues.

Tier 3

If the fight/flight system fails, we can just freeze. Dr. Porges says that this primordial response strategy is a complete shutdown or perhaps immobilization. This result is a relic from our invertebrate past. It works through the vagus nerve department that lacks a protective coating of myelin, the oily substance covering most nerves in mammals, enabling faster transmission of impulses.

The theory suggests that smiles, gentle eye contact, and soft voices with rhythmic inflections signal the brain structures that regulate the vagus nerve's myelinated pathway. His theory fits with several versions of psychological attachment theory, wherever it's believed that our connection with others is formed when we're babies, based on the style of nurturing we receive. Possibly the earlier we start and the more we practice staying in the social engagement system, the unlikely it's to switch off.

Our response to danger and the mobilization of primitive defensive systems, instead of the social engagement system, happens out of our conscious awareness. Our feelings of tension build approximately a point where our much more advanced system switches off, and the older mechanisms automatically take over.

But Dr. Porges says there is a way to help ourselves get to the social engagement system if our panic button is pressed. He says that we can find out to restore community engagement by inducing a calm behavioral state. We can relocate to a quiet room or even attempt to reconnect with others.

Social interactions are necessary for our experience as individuals, and the social engagement system determines the quality of those interactions. Calm behavioral states in others can induce similar states in individuals who would probably be struggling. A calm therapist can induce an equivalent state in a client through limbic resonance. Dr. Porges maintains that the social engagement system is compromised in people with autism and many psychiatric disorders.

Dr. Porges says that strategies as exercise tackle stress primarily at the visceral level; however, they can work against the operation of the bigger social engagement system. We've been taught that exercise is curative, but the calming effects we induce could be because of an analgesic effect on stress instead of a preventative effect. The aroused, excited state caused by exercise might inhibit mindful social engagement.

Polyvagal Theory and just how It Relates to Social Cues

Have you been in a situation where you feel uncertain or perhaps in danger but not sure why? You might be around and find out that nobody else appears to be bothered, but one thing still feels off to you?

You might not recognize it, but you're walking through the world every day, reading a huge number of social cues in your surroundings. In our interaction with others, we pick up facial expressions, tones of voice, physical movement, and much more. We're constantly busy interacting and observing with the planet and others included in the human experience.

As we have these contact with others, our sense of self has been shaped. We find out about ourselves and others, which we can believe in, which feels dangerous. Our bodies are processing this information type constantly through these interactions with the planet.

The Body's Surveillance System

Our central nervous system is an intricate structure that gathers info from all over our body and coordinates activity. You will find two primary neurological system areas: the central nervous system and the peripheral nervous system.

Central Nervous System

The central nervous system consists of two structures:

- Brain. This structure is composed of billions of interconnected neurons or perhaps nerve cells in the skull and functions as the coordinating center for nearly all of our body's functions. It's the seat of our intellect.

- Spinal cord. This is a bundled network of nerve fibers, connecting most parts of our body to our mind.

Peripheral Nervous System

The peripheral nervous system incorporates the nerves outside of our brain and spinal cord. It may be categorized into two distinct systems:

The somatic nervous system (voluntary). This system allows for our brains and muscles to communicate with one another. The somatic system will help our brain, and the spinal cord sends out signals to our muscles to enable them to move and send info from the body to the spinal cord and the brain.
The autonomic nervous system (involuntary). This system controls the glands and internal organs, like the heart, digestive system, and lungs. These are, basically, the things that run our body without us having to think about them deliberately. For instance, we can breathe and never having to consider taking a breath each time.

Reading Danger Cues

Our autonomic nervous system (the involuntary system, which helps control things like our breath, digestion, heart rate, and salivation) is complex and always busy. Along with running these essential functions in our bodies like helping us breathe, helping our heart pump, and helping us digest food, our autonomic nervous system helps us scan, interpret, and react to danger cues.

You will find two distinct systems at work within our autonomic nervous system, which are helping us to read and react to danger cues:

- Sympathetic nervous system. This product is needed to make our bodies react by mobilizing us to move when in dangerous situations. Many mention this particular system as prompting our "fight or perhaps flight" reactions to our surroundings' danger cues. It's also in charge of activating our adrenal glands to release epinephrine into our bloodstream, normally known as an adrenaline rush. When we stumble upon a snake, our sympathetic nervous system will read the possible threat's cue and prompt our body to respond, likely involving a quick adrenaline rush and us right away moving from the snake.

- Parasympathetic nervous system. This product is needed to calm our bodies, saving energy as it starts to do things like slow our heart rate, regulate our digestion, and minimize our blood pressure. Others refer to this particular system as the "rest and digest" system. As we start to read that a cue isn't deadly, our entire body starts to calm with the assistance of our parasympathetic nervous system.

The Vagus Nerve

There's one nerve, particularly, that's of interest to Dr. Stephen Porges, Ph.D. Dr. Porges is a notable faculty lecturer, scientist, and developer of what's described as the polyvagal theory. The vagus nerve will be the tenth cranial nerve, a quite long and wandering nerve that starts at the medulla oblongata. This particular brain component, the medulla oblongata, is situated in the lower part of the brain, sitting just above where the mind connects with our spinal cord.

You will find two sides to this vagus nerve, the dorsal (back) and the forward (front). From there, the sides of the vagus nerve run down throughout our body thought about having the widest distribution of all of the nerves within the body.

Scanning our environment from the precious time we're born, we're intuitively scanning our environment for cues of danger and safety.

We're wired for connection and, to be able to help us survive, our bodies are created and well prepared for observing, processing, and responding to our planet.

A baby responds to the secure feelings of closeness with their caregiver or perhaps a parent. Furthermore, a baby will respond to perceived as dangerous or scary cues, such as a stranger, a scary noise, or perhaps a lack of response from their caregiver. We scan for cues of danger and safety our whole lives.

Neuroception

In polyvagal theory, Dr. Porges explains the procedure in which our neural circuits are reading cues of threat in our environment as neuroception. Through this procedure of neuroception, we're delighting in the world and experiencing in a way where we're involuntarily scanning circumstances and individuals to decide whether they're unsafe or safe.

As a part of our autonomic nervous system, this procedure is going on without us even being informed it's occurring. Just as we're in a position to breathe and never having to intentionally tell ourselves to go for a breath, we're in a position to scan our environment for cues without telling ourselves to do it. The vagus nerve is of specific interest during this procedure of neuroception.

In the procedure of neuroception, both sides of our vagus nerve could be stimulated. Each side (dorsal ad ventral) has been found to respond in unique ways as we scan and process info from our social interactions and environment.

The forward (front) side of the vagus nerve responds to safety cues in our interactions and environment. It supports the sensations of physical safety and being securely emotionally linked to others in our environment.

The dorsal side of the vagus nerve reacts to cues of threat. It pulls us from connection, out of awareness, and into a state of self-protection. In moments when we could experience a hint of severe threat, we can close down and feel frozen, an indication that our dorsal vagal nerve has taken control.

3 Developmental Stages of Response

Within his polyvagal theory, Porges describes three evolutionary stages involved in advancing our autonomic nervous system. Instead of just suggesting that there's a balance between our sympathetic and parasympathetic nervous system, Porges describes that there's, in fact, a hierarchy of responses built into our autonomic nervous system.

Immobilization. Described as probably the oldest pathway, this involves an immobilization response. As you may remember, the dorsal (back) side of the vagus nerve responds to extreme danger cues, causing us to be immobile, which means that we will react to our fear by becoming shutting, numb, and frozen down. Almost as in the case, our parasympathetic nervous system is kicking into overdrive. Our response results in us freezing instead of merely slowing down.

Mobilization. Within this action, we've used our understanding nerve system, which, as you might recall, is the method that will assist us in mobilizing in the face of a danger hint. We take action with our adrenaline rush to leave from risk and even deal with our danger. Polyvagal theory recommends this path was next to evolve in the evolutionary hierarchy.

Social engagement. The newest inclusion to the hierarchy of responses is based on our ventral (front) side of the vagus nerve. Remembering that this particular component of the vagus nerve responds to feelings of connection and safety, social engagement allows us to feel anchored and is facilitated by that ventral vagus pathway. In this space, we can feel safe, connected, calm, and engaged.

The Response Hierarchy in Life that is daily

As we go through life engaging with the world, there are inevitably those moments when we will feel secure and others or perhaps in which we'll feel danger or discomfort. Polyvagal theory suggests this space is fluid for us, and we can go in and out of these various places within the hierarchy of responses.

We might encounter social engagement in the embrace of a safe loved one and, within the same day, find ourselves in mobilization as we're confronted with danger like a rabid dog, a robbery, or perhaps a rigorous conflict with a co-workers.

You will find occasions when we could read and respond to a danger cue and process the situation in a manner that leads us to feel unable and trapped to escape the circumstances. In those moments, our human body responds to increased feelings of distress and danger, moving into a primal space of immobilization. Our dorsal vagus nerve has been impacted and locking us down to a place of freezing, feeling numb, and, as some researchers believe, dissociation.

The danger cues can be way too overwhelming in those moments, and we see no viable way out. A good example of this might be moments of physical or sexual abuse.

Impact of Trauma

When someone has experienced trauma, especially in experiences wherever they had been left immobilized, their ability to scan their environment for danger cues can become skewed. Naturally, our body's goal is always to help us not experience a terrifying moment that way once again, so it will do whatever it has to do to help protect us.

As our surveillance system kicks in, working really tough to guard us, it can also read some cues in our environment as dangerous - even those cues that may be perceived as benign or neutral to other individuals.

Our social engagement allows us to have interact more fluidly with others, feeling connected and secure. When our body gets a cue within an interaction that signifies, we might not be safe, it begins to respond. For most, this cue may move them right into a mobilization response location, springing into action to attempt to neutralize the threat or perhaps get from the threat.

For those who have experienced an injury, the signal of a risk cue can move them straight from social engagement to immobilization. As they pertain to associate great deals of interpersonal cues as damaging, like a very little change of facial expression, a specific intonation, or maybe some type of body posturing, they could end up going to a location of action prevails to them to prepare and secure themselves.

The body doesn't authorize a response of mobilization as an option. This may be very difficult for trauma survivors, ignorant of exactly how this hierarchy of response is affected by their interactions with others and the world.

Connection and Polyvagal Theory

Although the vagus nerve is understood as commonly dispersed and attached to numerous body areas, you must know this system can affect cranial nerves controlling social engagement, facial expression, and vocalization. As individuals wired for connection, we can see how scanning for danger cues can often happen in our interactions with our significant other or perhaps important supportive others in our lives.

We innately look for feelings of safety, trust, and comfort in our connections with others and quickly pick up cues that show us when we might not be safe. As individuals start to be safer with and for one another, it could be easier to build experience intimacy, share vulnerabilities, and healthy bonds.

Chapter 10

Sleep Problems and the Vagus Nerve

Vagus Nerve Science for a much better Night's Sleep

Trouble sleeping leads to trouble doing essentially other things. The effects of not getting a sufficient amount of rest - or even high-quality rest - go beyond just feeling grumpy the following day. In reality, sleep deprivation is linked to several serious long term health consequences, including obesity, heart disease, a weakened immune system, and far more.

Thus, what might you do to fight sleep struggles and wake up feeling ready, healthy, and rested to go? It turns out, and the answer could lie in stimulating your vagus nerve.

The Vagus Nerve and restful sleep

What's the vagus nerve, you may be asking? To put it simply, it is probably the longest nerve of the autonomic nervous system. This system handles regulating a range of body processes that take place with no conscious effort. This could include breathing, social interaction, digestion, sweating, heart rate, and far more.

Additionally, it happens to be just about the most important nerves within the body. The vagus nerve is acquired from the

Latin term for "roaming." It starts at the brain and strolls near the ear canal then into almost every major organ system.

The vagus nerve can be strongly connected with sleep quality. It balances the central nervous system by promoting a relaxation response, a crucial element of good sleep.

Under perfect conditions, your body sends autonomic signals, including increased parasympathetic (vagal) activity and reduced sympathetic drive before you fall asleep. This adds to your heart rate decreasing. As you can envision, a reduced heart rate induces a state of relaxation, and ultimately sleep.

Nevertheless, you can wrestle with an assortment of sleep disorders and sleep deprivation if your vagus nerve is not properly stimulated. Maybe you simply do not get adequate hours of sleep, or perhaps you cannot fall right into a deep sleep, in case you can drift off at all.

That is exactly where vagus nerve stimulation (VNS) comes in. Study shows that stimulating the vagus nerve can dramatically affect your general well-being, including adding to a much better night's sleep!

Thus, you understand that your vagus nerve should be stimulated to allow you to drift off and improve sleep quality. But how can you do that?

The way to stimulate the vagus nerve science for a much better night's sleep

VNS has been scientifically researched for decades because of its power to greatly improve sleep and several other functions.

The vagus nerve's electrical stimulation sends messages to the brain to produce calming sensations to the body. While this modern method is today that is available, VNS is not a new idea. In reality, individuals have practiced forms of vagus nerve stimulation for centuries. Meditation, chanting, yoga, and mindfulness are several practices that provide indirect stimulation to the vagus nerve.

It may sound easy, but some find that amount of relaxation difficult to achieve.

Enter auricular (ear based) vagus nerve stimulation.
Auricular (ear based) vagus nerve stimulation is an effective and safe method of neurostimulation. Research has been done on both healthy subjects and those battling chronic conditions, including sleep disorders.

Utilizing current technology, the vagus nerve could be activated in several various ways. Probably the most attainable, minimally invasive option is referred to as tVNS (transcutaneous VNS).

tVNS utilizes electrical stimulation through the surface area of the skin. It is frequently done via the left ear but can additionally be accomplished on the neck. The user tries the tVNS themselves, and it does not require surgery or perhaps other procedure. tVNS is an approachable way to promote and maintain wellness and health in general, including promoting better sleep quality.

Auricular VNS falls under the tVNS category. It delivers electrical stimulation to the vagus nerve (ABVN), which happens to be the only peripheral branch of the vagus nerve. This makes for an easily available target within the human ear!

Ear-based vagus nerve activation has been successfully studied in many people, for numerous reasons. They include mood, athletic performance recovery, and cognition, focus, and sleep.

Nowadays, researchers are focusing a lot more on the advantages of ear-based tVNS and its potential to have a proper sense of balance in the neurological system and, to the possible extent, mitigating the consequences of chronic conditions.

Sleep deprivation

We spend a third of our life sleeping. There ought to be the right reason why nature makes us sleep for this long. A huge number of studies around the globe have proven the good beneficial effects of sleep.

On the other hand, sleep deprivation results in impairment of judgment, heart problems, depression, obesity, and a drastic reduction in an individual's well-being. In a serious case, sleep deprivation has also resulted in death through heart failure. In reality, the very first sign of sickness is fretful sleep.

How lack of sleep can help make you ill

How lack of sleep produces ill-health has remained a mystery. Today, slowly, scientific investigations are solving this puzzle.

Among the accepted theories up to now has been that sleep aids in both removal and consolidation of memories. We see the world during the day through our feelings, resulting in memory formation, deep and shallow. Sleep, it seems, helps in consolidating and taking away several of these memories uncluttering the brain.

Another current but interesting theory (backed with experiments) has proven that sleep aids in flushing out toxic protein waste and natural debris from the brain, formed during waking hours. It appears that during sleep, the relaxation of the brain will help in opening up the channels whereby the debris flows into the bloodstreams and is removed from it.

Scientific studies also have proven that sleep helps flush out harmful protein plaque (beta-amyloid) that is liable for neurodegenerative diseases as Alzheimer's and dementia. Thus good sleep is essential for a healthy body and brain.

The build-up of toxins in the brain as a result of insufficient sleep also impacts the body. Though there's almost no knowledge of how this happens, a probable cause is the passage of the info by the vagus nerve to various body areas.

Scientific investigations also have found that info of any small change in the brain chemistry is transmitted to various organs by the vagus nerve, which plays an immensely important part in maintaining the mind and body in unison.

As the brain starts getting impacted by the debris build-up, the message through the vagus nerve to different organs may slow them down, resulting in their slow action.

Meditation can help.

Much like deep sleep, meditation also enables the dissolution of memories. In reality, deep meditation and sleep have similar qualities, and it's very probable that during meditation, the flushing of toxins from the brain may also occur.

A possible system could be that given that meditation results in the brain's relaxation, it might help open up the channels for flushing off the chemical particles.

Memory is formed both by producing brand-new neural pathways and certain chemical changes in the human brain. Memory removal, for that reason, is impacted by modifications in both these systems.

In deep meditation (where the focus is on one thought for a while, likewise, called Sanyam), new neural pathways are formed, and likewise, the older ones get dissolved. This dissolution might have a chemical signature, thereby producing toxic particles, which have been flushed out.

Just how can we induce good sleep?

1. Generally, once the body is good and the person follows a great workout regime, this helps produce deep sleep.

2. Production of deep sleep may also be helped by meditation. Studies world over have found that long-term practice of meditation helps in toning both the mind and body.

3. A very good meditation practice to follow for quickly dropping off to sleep is always to close the eyes and focus attention on the center of the forehead. This is usually done just before going to sleep and when one wakes up at night and has difficulty dropping off to sleep again.

Tone Your Vagus Nerve to Sleep Better

Trouble sleeping can interfere with lucid dreaming. A sufficient level of rest is needed for lucid dreaming since you get much of your REM sleep, the stage of sleep when lucid dreams are likely to occur in the second half of the night. A refreshed body and mind will help you concentrate on inducing and keeping lucid dreams.

Improving sleep health and stimulus control and developing sleep-promoting ideas and habits can allow you to get the best sleep possible. Some sleep conditions and psychiatric conditions can mimic or possibly intensify insomnia, so it is also important to identify and treat them if you're having a problem sleeping. Learning deep relaxation skills is one more potent way that will help you drift to sleep fast, particularly skills that effectively target the vagus nerve.

Your Vagus Nerve

Your mind and body are very relaxed and best positioned for falling into a restful sleep when your vagus nerve is activated.

The vagus nerve is probably the longest of your twelve cranial nerves, running from the brain through the center to the gut. It's noted for its role in your digestion," and "rest or perhaps parasympathetic, central nervous system." It also regulates various bodily systems like breathing, digestion, heart rate, and social behaviors.

The vagus nerve has an evolutionarily older element called the "dumb" vagus that influences dissociation, immobilization, or possibly "freeze" actions. The current part of the vagus, called the "smart" vagus, helps you down-regulate stress and effectively engage in social interactions. The smart vagus circuit can be reinforced willingly to improve your capacity for relationship and self-regulation with others. Exercising your vagus nerve and enhancing vagal "tone" can make you versatile and adaptive in responding to your environments' cues. By "toning" your central nervous system, you can buffer against stress and recover quicker from it.

Heart Rate Variability

Your vagal tone can be calculated by a rhythm in your heart, referred to as heart rate variability. Heart rate variability isn't like your heart rate. Rather, it's an index of the periods between your heart beats.

All individuals have an arrhythmia in their heart rate patterns: your heart rate speeds up if you breathe in and slows if you breathe out (also known as respiratory sinus arrhythmia). The bigger and smoother these waveforms in your heart rhythm are, the greater your vagus nerve is activated, and also, the more relaxed you'll feel.

When you experience stress - ranging from major life challenges to daily problem solving - these waveforms be erratic and compressed. Supported compression of heart rate variability is generally a marker of poorer health and general functioning.

Unfortunately, the stress in a modern society tends to be chronic, and lots of folks stay stuck in a low vagal tone, which doesn't help them sleep well, and far less, vivaciously thrive in the world.

But by improving your heart rate variability, your vagus nerve becomes more activated and responsive. This can help you handle all types of life issues improved, such as your ability to drift off quickly and deeply.

Resonant Frequency Breath Training

Breathing with your diaphragm at a slow rate and rhythm can enhance just how much your heart rate accelerates and decelerates with each breath, improving the tone of your vagus nerve.

A lot of people breathe between 12 to 20 breaths per minute. With this particular technique, you slow your breathing rate to approximately six breaths per minute. This creates a resonance effect between your blood pressure, breathing, and heart rate, maximizing your heart rate variability.

This state often induces a sensation of ease, relaxation, a loosening of muscle tension, and in case you're sleep deprived sleepiness. It may be practiced intermittently in the day to reduce your baseline levels of stress so that as you strengthen your vagal tone, it may be put on to soothe and calm yourself when needed. The more you exercise this breathing technique, the better and wiser this reflex of your vagus nerve will become.

Here is how you can learn this technique.

Breathe Like a Baby

The first action to learn resonant frequency breathing is to train yourself to breathe with your diaphragm, so your abdomen stretches with the inhale and flattens with the exhale.

Have you ever seen a newborn breathe? Infants don't yet possess the ability to breathe shallowly in their chests since they lack tone in their accessory breathing muscles. Thus, babies breathe entirely using their diaphragm, the muscle that separates your chest and abdominal cavities and assists you to breathe automatically.

Most parents are likely to chronically breathe shallowly in their chests. This is an all-natural response to navigating higher levels of stress as well as activity in life. Nevertheless, folks still chest breathe no matter if they are not facing major stressors, making their recovery from life's challenges slower or perhaps even absent.

Place a hand on your chest as well as one on your belly, and inhale. Does your chest rise if you breathe in? Or perhaps is your breath more centered on your diaphragm, so your belly inflates when you inhale?

To breathe with your diaphragm, allowing the air to get into all of the ways to the soles of your lungs so that your diaphragm pushes your belly out if you breathe in and allows your belly to deflate when you breathe out. Make certain your chest stays completely still as you breathe abdominally.

For approximately one week, practice this for ten minutes each day. Do this without delaying the pace of your breath just yet.

Paced Breathing

When you're confident with diaphragmatic breathing, gradually slow your breathing rate until it reaches approximately six breaths per minute. This means you'll ultimately find out to inhale for five seconds and exhale for five seconds. Or perhaps, you can inhale for four seconds and exhale for six seconds.

Some find it much more comfortable or perhaps relaxing to breathe at a slower or faster slightly rate than six breaths per minute. Experiment with different rates to get a pace that matches your needs. But remember that, on average, the majority of folks achieve a state of resonance when breathing at six breaths per minute.

If you've trouble slowing your breathing pace, then slow it just about where you're comfortable. With practice and time, you can comfortably and gradually achieve a slower pace until you're breathing at a rate of ~ six breaths/minute.

Practice for no less than ten minutes consecutively every day.

Use Breath Pacers

A visual or perhaps audio pacer can help you focus on pacing your breathing better than counting the lengths of exhalations and inhalations. For visual pacers, breathe in when the pacer ascends or possibly expands and breathes out when the pacer descends or maybe decreases. Inhale when the tones ascend and breathe out when the tones descend if you utilize an audio pacer.

There will also be home training biofeedback devices, like the emWave device, by Heart Math, which will help you target and maximize your heart rate variability with increased accuracy.

Breath pacers are great training tools. But eventually, you will want to have the ability to pace your breathing intuitively all by yourself, so you can easily use this skill if needed.

Paced Breathing to Induce Sleep

When you're attempting to drift off, apply the process of paced breathing at ~ six breaths per minute. When this is used in the context of good sleep habits, it can enable you to drift off faster.

Couple this technique with meditating on your feelings, like your breath, without judging your experience. This can help you stay away from thinking of things, which can activate your brain and make it more difficult to fall asleep. Put simply, and you can induce positive, bottom-up (paced breathing) and top-down (meditation) influences on your nervous system to eliminate or perhaps reduce insomnia.

Daytime Diaphragmatic Breathing

It's ideal to set a minimum of ten minutes apart to formally practice paced diaphragmatic breathing during the day. This could reset, balance, and tone your nervous system in ways that positively influence your overall ability to navigate reality.

It can additionally help partake in a much less setup practice of diaphragmatic breathing. This works by becoming mindful of your breath multiple times each day and shifting your breath from your chest to the abdomen. You can do this at idle points, each time you think of it, or even if you notice your levels of stress and arousal are higher. Feel free to also slow your breath's pace, if that is okay, for no less than a couple of breaths.

This down-regulation of the central nervous system can reduce your baseline levels of stress and hyperarousal. This not only helps your decision making and functioning while awake, but it can help make it simpler to downshift into a state of restful sleep after the day.

Trouble-Shooting

Paced diaphragmatic breathing comes quicker to some than others. Dedicating to the practice and being a client can make your learning procedure smoother.

The following are several issues frequently observed in those new to the strategy and how you can defeat them. Specialists that offer heart rate irregularity biofeedback treatment in your area may likewise have the capability to help you.

Light-headedness

Many people feel lightheaded when they begin practicing paced breathing. If this happens to you, be sure that you're lying down when you practice. It also can certainly help to purse your lips if you breathe out to fight some dizziness. This feeling could eventually disappear with training, and breathing with your diaphragm will feel easy and naturally more.

You cannot breathe abdominally.

You may learn it's way too difficult for you to breathe so that your abdomen rises on the inhale rather than your chest. Nevertheless, you must realize that you already breathe with your diaphragm every time you're in deeply relaxed states, like when you're falling or asleep after eating a huge meal.

If you are still having trouble, do not give up. Instead, try practicing when you're lying down flat and currently in a relaxed state. You are going to see that you naturally breathe abdominally when you're naturally relaxed. When you feel far more positive in your ability to breathe this way, apply the skill in different situations too.

You do not feel relaxed.

More than likely, you're not exercising paced breathing enough. Your vagal reflex is similar to a muscle. You have to exercise it repetitively and regularly for it to get stronger. The thumb rule is usually to practice paced diaphragmatic breathing a minimum of ten consecutive minutes each day. While this is typically sufficient to do the trick, sometimes folks call for twenty minutes of daily practice to notice results.

Additionally, you may find out it is tough for you to remember to practice for long, or perhaps to find the time to practice at all. If so, try scheduling this practice at points, you will be more likely to do it, like at bedtime. You can also split your ten-minute goal into smaller chunks of time throughout the day. Doing a couple of minutes occasionally is much more helpful than not training at all.

Additionally, you might not be doing the skill correctly. A frequently seen error is just doing this method when you're stressed to calm yourself down, which does not work nicely if you have not mastered the skill yet. Rather, you need to practice when you're actually in a fairly relaxed state, allowing you to stretch and strengthen this response in your vagus nerve best. Once this reflex gets better, you will induce relaxation quickly whenever you use the skill, including when you're much more stressed.

Take-Home Points

To lucid dream, you have to sleep easily and deeply and get adequate sleep. In case you have difficulty with insomnia, a powerful technique for inducing relaxation and sleep is to train the rhythms of your vagus nerve, which is accountable for relaxing your body and head.

Activating your vagus nerve is possible through several relaxation techniques. Compared with most regular relaxation techniques, diaphragmatic breathing at a six breaths/minute pace is much more effective at targeting and maximizing vagal activity, therefore, inducing states of sleep and relaxation. This is because paced breathing develops a resonance impact in your heart rate variability, an index of your vagal tone.

The method is discovered most efficiently through expert biofeedback therapies. Your learning may likewise be self-guided through education, breathing pacers, and constant practice.

Chapter 11

Activating the Vagus Nerve

Good vagal nerve function is vital for optimum health. Emerging research indicates that it may not function very well in several chronic disease states. This chapter will review factors that could increase its tone with stimulation and just how this could impact health.

When to See a Doctor

Suppose your aim is usually to stimulate your vagus nerve to improve your mood or perhaps extreme stress-related issues, including panic disorders or perhaps anxiety. In that case, you must speak to your doctor, especially about stress, if it is significantly impacting your everyday life.

Major mental changes, for example, too much sadness, panic, persistent low mood, or anxiety, euphoria, are many reasons to visit a doctor.

Your doctor ought to identify and treat any underlying conditions causing your symptoms.

Keep in mind that the current evidence doesn't suggest that low vagal tone causes mood or anxiety disorders. Problems that are complex as anxiety always involve multiple possible factors, including brain chemistry, health status, environment, and genetics that may differ from one person to another.

Furthermore, changes in nerve tone and brain chemistry aren't things that individuals can change by themselves with the approaches listed here. Rather, the elements mentioned in this article are intended to reduce daily stress and support overall mental health and well-being. Most are backed up just by limited human or perhaps animal studies.

Thus, you might try the strategies listed below if you and your doctor determine that they might be appropriate. Read through the methods we bring up and talk about them with your physician before trying them out. This is very vital in case you intend to take any dietary supplements.

The FDA hasn't accredited supplements for medical use and generally lack solid medical research. Regulations set manufacturing standards for them but do not ensure they are effective or safe.

Lastly, have in mind that not one of these strategies should be done in place of what your doctor recommends or perhaps prescribes.

Factors that could Stimulate the Vagus Nerve

1) Cold

According to one study on ten healthy folks, once the body adjusts to cool temperatures, your fight-or-flight (sympathetic) system declines. Your rest-and-digest (parasympathetic) system increases mediated by the vagus nerve. In this study, temperatures of 50F (10C) were considered cold.

Sudden cold exposure (39F/4C) also increases vagus nerve activation in rats.

Even though cold showers' effects on vagus nerve tone have not been studied, many folks advocate for this traditional cooling method.

When we consider it, all showers were cold showers before the advent of water heating techniques. Anecdotally, cold tubs are common in Japan, while many Northern nations partake in dips in the ocean for special occasions during early spring or the winter.

It typically takes some time to get used to fully cool showers, however. Many people say it is great to dip your face in water that is cool for beginners.

Remember to consult your healthcare provider first, however. Most physicians recommend cold showers in individuals with cardiovascular disease or perhaps in those at risk. That is since unexpected cold exposure can restrict capillary, which may raise heart rate and high blood pressure.

Cold exposure might stimulate the vagus nerve and rest-and-digest system.

2) Chanting or singing

According to an experiment on healthy 18-year-olds, singing increases heart rate variability (HRV).

Heart rate variability continues to be connected with relaxation, improved stress resilience and adaptation, and higher rest-and-digest (parasympathetic) activity.

The mentioned study writers found humming, hymn singing, mantra chanting, and upbeat, energetic singing all increase HRV in somewhat different ways.

They hypothesized that singing starts the work of a vagal pump, sending relaxing waves through the choir.

Additionally, singing at the top part of your lungs might work the muscles in the throat's rear to activate the vagus.

On the other hand, this study's writers think that energetic singing activates both the sympathetic nervous system and vagus nerve, which may help folks get right into a movement state.

Singing in unison, which is frequently done in synagogues and churches, also increased HRV and vagus function in this study.

Nevertheless, no other similar reports have been carried out. The above-discussed study included only 15 healthy 18-year-olds. We do not understand how different singing and chanting types affect the vagus nerve in folks of various ages or even suffering from mental health issues. Larger studies are necessary.

In one other study dealing with this connection, singing was found to increase oxytocin in amateur and professional singers.

Both groups felt stimulated after a singing session; however, amateur vocalists stated they sense greater well-being and less arousal than professionals. The authors pointed out that this could be because amateurs approached singing as a relaxation and self-realization technique, while the professionals were achievement-oriented.

Thus, you might wish to relax and express yourself almost as possible when chanting and singing. Try never to consider how you sound and whether you will reach the objectives you set for that session.

Chanting, energetic singing, and choral singing may indirectly stimulate the vagus nerve, particularly in an unwillingness to unwind during the sessions.

3) Yoga

Scientific studies that are Limited suggest a link between yoga and increased vagus parasympathetic system activity and nerve in common.

A 12-week yoga intervention was more powerful related to enhancements in stress and anxiety and state of mind than strolling exercises, which worked as the control group. The study found increased thalamic GABA levels that are connected with improved mood and decreased anxiety.

Yoga is believed to be great for supporting overall physical and mental health. More research is needed on its results on the vagus nerve tone.

4) Meditation

Research suggests that a minimum of three kinds of meditation may stimulate the vagus nerve indirectly. In small studies, Om, mindfulness meditation, and loving-kindness meditation chanting increased heart rate variability, which happens to be associated with vagal tone.

Some researchers think conscious, deep breathing that accompanies meditation and other reflective practices might underlie this impact. Mindful breathing is assumed to directly promote the vagus nerve and rest-and-digest nervous activity.

Larger studies and more human studies on numerous kinds of meditation are needed.

5) Positive Thoughts and Social Connection

In a study of sixty-five folks, one-half of the participants had been told to sit and think compassionately about others by silently repeating phrases like "May you feel safe," "may you feel happy," "may you feel healthy," "may you live with ease," and keep returning to these thoughts when their minds wandered.

As compared to the controls, the meditators showed a general increase in positive, serenity, amusement, interest, joy, and hope after the class. These psychological and emotional changes have been correlated with a much better sense of connectedness to others and improved vagal function, as seen by heart rate variability.

Simply meditating, nonetheless, did not always lead to a far more toned vagus nerve. The change just occurred in meditators, who became happier and felt much more socially connected. Those who meditated saw it as significant but did not report feeling any better to others who showed no change in the vagus nerve's tone.

Although much more study is needed, these findings suggest that the vagus nerve is tied to how social connections and positive emotions may help folks on a path to better health.

Social connection and positive thoughts may stimulate the vagus nerve and promote compassion, serenity, and joy.

6) Deep and Slow Breathing

Deep and slow breathing is assumed to promote the vagus nerve, and it is very likely typical of numerous types of relaxation, meditation, and yoga techniques.

Your heart and neck consist of neurons that have receptors called baroreceptors.

These specialized nerve cells spot high blood pressure and transfer the neuronal signal to the brain (NTS). If a person's high blood pressure is high, this signal activates their vagus nerve, which links to the center to lower blood pressure and heart rate.

Baroreceptors can be variably sensitive. Some scientists believe that the more vulnerable they are, the more apt they are gonna fire and tell the brain that the blood pressure is way too high, and it is time to activate the vagus nerve to lower it.

One study tested the effects of slow yogic breathing called ujjayi, which could be performed at different breathing rates in and outside, on seventeen healthy individuals. With a roughly equivalent quantity of time breathing in and out, ujjayi breathing increased the sensitivity of vagal activation and baroreceptors, which reduced high blood pressure.

This particular kind of slow breathing involved six breaths per minute, approximately five seconds per inhale, five seconds per exhale.

Some researchers think that slow yogic breathing may reduce anxiety by reducing the sympathetic nervous system and increasing the parasympathetic system, but this has not been confirmed yet.

Tip: Yoga practitioners point out you have to breathe from your belly, slowly. This means if you inhale, your stomach should broaden in addition to go external. Your stubborn belly needs to cave in when you breathe out. The more your stubborn belly expands, and it caves in, the greater you are breathing.

Slow and deep breathing may boost vagus nerve activity and relaxation. Yogis say you need to try to breathe from your belly at approximately six breaths per minute.

7) Laughter

There might be a bit of fact to the saying laughter is the perfect medicine. A couple of research studies suggest the health benefits of laughing.

Researchers suggest that laughter may be able to stimulate the vagus nerve, claiming that laughter therapy is something that could be effective for health. Still, studies continue to be numerous, and it is difficult to say precisely how and why laughter makes us feel very good.

A study done on yoga laughter discovered increased HRV (heart rate irregularity) in the laughter group.

Nevertheless, you will find numerous case reports of folks fainting from laughter. Doctors mention that this might be from the vagus nerve/parasympathetic system being stimulated too much.

For instance, some research suggests that fainting can come after laughter, urination, coughing, swallowing, or perhaps bowel movements, all of which are helped by vagus activation.

You will find case reports of folks passing out from laughter who have a rare syndrome (Angelman's) connected with increased vagus stimulation.

At times, laughter is a complication of vagus nerve stimulation performed with special devices in kids with epilepsy.

Some researchers would like to determine whether an excellent bout of laughter will work for cognitive function and heart disease protection. Limited scientific studies suggest that laughter increases nitric oxide and beta-endorphins, which theoretically benefit the vascular system.

Laughing may activate the vagus nerve and have additional health benefits, but overdoing it may cause fainting in rare cases.

8) Prayer

One little study found that reciting the rosary prayer may increase vagus activation. Particularly, it seemed to improve cardiovascular rhythms, reducing diastolic high blood pressure, and increasing HRV.

According to one research study group, the reading of one rosary cycle takes around ten seconds, causing readers to breathe at 10-second intervals (includes both in and out-breath), which increases HRV and, therefore, vagus function.

Prayer deepens and slows breathing, which tends to stimulate the vagus nerve.

9) PEMF

Some scientists assume that electromagnetic fields might have the ability to promote the vagus nerve. In a report on thirty healthy males, pulsed electromagnetic field (PEMF) therapy increases heart rate variability and vagus stimulation. Nevertheless, no other scientific studies have replicated these findings.

PEMF devices are classified as general health products. The FDA hasn't accredited them for dealing with some problems.

PEMF therapy may increase vagus nerve activity, but more research is required.

10) Probiotics

Emerging evidence points to an outcome of the gut microbiota on the human brain. The gut's nervous system links to the brain through the vagus nerve, described as the microbiota-gut-brain axis interface.

Some animal studies have looked at the likely effects of probiotics on the vagus nerve, but clinical trials continue to be lacking.

In an animal experiment, mice supplemented with the probiotic Lactobacillus rhamnosus experienced various positive changes in GABA receptors that had been mediated by the vagus nerve.

GABA receptors in the brain are connected in mood; a possible link between vagus nerve gut stimulation by L. rhamnosus and enhanced GABA activity adds to a body of emerging evidence about probiotics' possible health benefits.

11) Exercise

Does mild exercise stimulate gut flow in animals? And vagus nerve activation was needed to begin this response. Consequently, some scientists hypothesize that exercise may stimulate the vagus nerve, although there is no human evidence to support this theory.

12) Massage

Massaging certain parts like the carotid sinus (located on your neck) can stimulate the vagus nerve. The study indicates that it might help reduce seizures (note: massaging a carotid sinus isn't recommended at home as a result of other risks) as well as possible fainting

A pressure massage may also stimulate the vagus nerve. These messages helped infants gain weight by stimulating the gut, which is largely mediated by vagus nerve activation.

According to a small study on individuals who are good and patients with cardiovascular disease, reflexology foot massages are claimed to increase vagal activity and heart rate variability while lowering heart rate and blood pressure.

Neck, foot, and pressure massages may activate the vagus nerve.

13) Fasting

Intermittent fasting and reducing calories increase heart rate variability in animals, which is believed to be a vagal tone marker.

Several individuals claim intermittent fasting boosted their heart rate variability, but no clinical trials can vouch for this effect.

According to some theory, the vagus nerve might mediate a decrease in metabolism upon fasting. Particularly, the vagus detects a decline in the decrease and blood glucose of the gut's chemical and mechanical stimuli. According to animal data, this appears to increase vagus impulses from the liver to the brain (NTS), which slows the metabolism.

Animal studies suggest that hormones like NPY increase while CRH and CCK decrease during fasting.

The complete opposite may occur after eating. Satiety-related stimulatory signals from the gut seem to contribute to increased sympathetic activity and stress responsiveness (higher CRH, CCK, minimizing NPY).

The vagus nerve may make animals much more sensitive to estrogen when they're hungry. In female rats, fasting escalates the number of estrogen receptors in some brains (PVN and NTS), mediated by the vagus nerve.

Fasting may delay metabolism by promoting vagus nerve activity.

14) Laying or Sleeping on Your Right Side

Limited scientific studies suggest that laying on your right side increases heart rate variability and vagal activation over getting on your other side. Laying on the back led to probably the lowest vagus activation in one study. More research is required.

15) Tai Chi

In a single study on sixty-one folks, tai chi increased heart rate variability and, consequently, likely vagus activation.

16) Seafood (DHA) and EPA

A few scientific reviews reported omega-3 essential fatty acids DHA and EPA increase heart rate variability (HRV) and reduced heart rate. HRV is directly connected to vagus nerve stimulation.

Some experts think that vagus nerve activity might explain why omega-3 essential fatty acids are great for the heart, but more research is required.

Furthermore, fish is a crucial part of the lectin avoidance diet.

17) Zinc

Zinc improved vagus stimulation in rats fed a zinc-deficient diet for three days. It is a really common mineral that some individuals do not get enough of.

18) Acupuncture

Based on limited research, traditional acupuncture points may stimulate the vagus nerve, particularly those on the ears.

Acupuncture might not be safe. A male died after vagus nerve stimulation from way too small of a heart rate in a single report. Be sure to work with a qualified acupuncture practitioner and let your physician know in case you intend to see an acupuncturist.

19) Eating Fiber

GLP-1 is a satiating hormone that triggers vagus impulses to the brain, reducing the gut movements and making us feel fuller after meals.

Animal research proposes that fiber may be a great method to increase GLP 1 [forty-four].

Sun Exposure

We do not yet know whether sun exposure can stimulate the vagus nerve, although this is theoretically possible.

Alpha-MSH prevents destruction from a stroke in rats by activating the vagus nerve, which suppresses inflammation.

Alpha-MSH injection in the brain (DMV) moderately awakens the vagus nerve in some conditions.

Exposure to the sun is hypothesized to naturally boost alpha MSH, but it will be a long stretch to say that sun exposure can stimulate the vagus nerve. Future studies will have to explore this.

Experimental (Lacking Evidence)

The next factors are anecdotal or theoretical. They are not supported by sound science, and they're not generally associated with well-being. We recommend against them but think they are interesting to point out for informational purposes.

Gargling

The vagus nerve stimulates the muscles in the rear of the throat that allows you to gargle.

Hypothetically speaking, gargling contracts these muscles, triggering the vagus nerve and promoting the intestinal tract.

Tongue Depressors

Tongue depressors promote the gag reflex. The vagus nerve is straight linked to the muscles on the back of the throat that manage this reflex.

Others point out that gag reflexes are like doing push-ups for the vagus nerve while gargling and singing loudly are like making sprints. However, there is no good science to back this up.

Chewing Gum

CCK (a gut hormone) appears to immediately activate vagal impulses in the human brain.

The capability of CCK to reduce appetite and food intake is determined by the vagus nerve impulses back and forth from the human brain.

Chewing gum may increase CCK release, but most gum isn't healthy and contains other additives and artificial sweeteners.

Tensing or perhaps coughing the Stomach Muscles

When you bear down (as if to create a bowel movement), you might manage to mechanically stimulate your vagus nerve. Some even state that this is why folks feel relaxed after a bowel movement. Nevertheless, science is lacking to suggest that simulating bowel movements will stimulate the vagus nerve.

Alpha-GPC (Acetylcholine)

No studies suggest that alpha GPC stimulates the vagus nerve. Many people think it might, since it may increase acetylcholine, which is the main vagal neurotransmitter.

This implies that it may, in theory, have effects on vagal stimulation, but we do not know if this comes about when someone takes alpha GPC supplements.

Enemas

Expanding the bowel improves vagus nerve stimulation. Enemas expand the bowel, but they bring many risks when they are not used under medical supervision. Using enemas at home could be especially dangerous. Regular use can cause severe electrolyte imbalances and death.

Potential Inhibitors

These are all experimental. No human trials exist to determine exactly how these compounds affect the vagus nerve in humans. Below is a summary of the existing cell and animal-based research, which ought to guide further investigational efforts.

One) Carbohydrates (Insulin)

Insulin, which the body releases after meals, controls the part of the vagus nerve innervating the liver. Increased insulin levels seen in obesity may compromise the vagus nerve's normal function, and consequently, the liver, but more research is required.

Two) Capsaicin

In animal studies, capsaicin is thought to be the most powerful (and spicy) way to inhibit the vagus nerve. No evidence eating spicy, capsaicin-rich foods blocks the vagus nerve in humans, however.

Three) Ginger

Ginger is hypothesized to prevent vomiting and nausea by inhibiting the vagus nerve and serotonin function in the intestinal tract. We do not know whether eating ginger reduces the vagus nerve activity. Generally speaking, ginger is a healthy spice, and there is no reason to stay away from it unless directed by your physician.

Takeaway

The vagus nerve plays a central role in the rest-and-digest (parasympathetic) nervous system.

Factors that could stimulate the vagus nerve naturally include yoga, fasting, singing, cold exposure, prayer, meditation, and massage. Nutrients and supplements explored for boosting vagus nerve activity include probiotics, zinc, fiber, and omega-three fatty acids. The study continues to be limited. Make sure you consult a physician before taking supplements or perhaps making major lifestyle changes.

Chapter 12

Treating the Vagus Nerve

The vagus nerve is the core of the mind-body connection. Signals which are carried from the gut and organs via the vagus nerve influence the entire brain. These messages affect how you feel, and subliminal decisions are made from these signals that can greatly affect your actions.

Amongst the techniques to calculate exactly how the vagus nerve functions are by assessing your heart rate variability. Heart rate irregularity refers to the oscillations of your heart rate, which accompany the breath.

Higher heart rate variability is related to an even greater potential to recover from tough circumstances. On the contrary, lower heart rate variability is associated with emotional dysregulation, anxiety, and prolonged stress that carries on after a situation that was difficult for us has ended.

Using the vagus nerve, you can enhance your heart rate variability and build resilience and flexibility within your autonomic nervous system.

In case you think of a recent stressful event, you might ask yourself:

• Just how long did it take for me to go back to a state of calm after I was stressed?

- Did the quantity of fear/anxiety/stress/ anger that came up for me appropriately match this scenario?

- Am I usually experiencing a feeling of worry or perhaps fear, although I know things are ok rationally?

- Do I get gastrointestinal issues after stress?

- Do I experience insomnia in difficult times?

Mental health is as well a base of your physical health. There's a flow-on impact of your mental states to your immune system, digestive system, your lungs and heart, sleep, as well as your capability to connect with others. Chronic emotional states can age you faster!

Including tools and techniques that balance your central nervous system via the vagus nerve won't just enhance your long term digestive health, mental health, and immunity. Additionally, it will help you to forge richer and far more long-lasting connections with others.

In time and with the appropriate equipment, it could get less difficult to move between feelings of anxiety and fear to a state of ease and calm. It's likely to relieve depression and anxiety, gastrointestinal issues, chronic pain, and sleep disturbances when you use your vagus nerve.

Transcutaneous vagus nerve stimulation, acupuncture, and mind-body neural practices can regulate pro-inflammatory cytokines launched by the neurological system under tension and dampen the inflammatory action. The stimulation process to the vagus nerve, or perhaps improving vagal tone, influences the markers of inflammation.

Acupuncture inhibits the synthesis of tumor necrosis factor and evokes the activity of the vagus nerve. The acupuncture points in the suboccipital auricular (neck region and ear) are located in the nerve distribution area and affect the vagus nerve. Among the advantages of using acupuncture to stimulate the vagus nerve is surgery-free and risk- and does not produce any bad side effects.

The vagus nerve is probably the longest in our body and connects the brain with many important organs, like the intestines, stomach, heart, and lungs. The vagus nerve is an immensely important component of the parasympathetic' rest & digest' nervous system. It is the nerve that influences your breathing, digestive function, and heart rate, ultimately affecting your mental health.

Additionally, you have to pay particular focus to the tone of your vagus nerve, which refers to the natural process that encourages and triggers the vagus nerve's activity. If this vagal tone increases, it is going to activate the parasympathetic nervous system. This means that having a higher vagal tone means you can relax sooner, even when under stress.

Although this vagal tone is linked to inflammation, the immune system, emotional regulation, and metabolism, that is crucial to our body. This means the vagus nerve has been connected with mental health conditions, like anxiety. Low vagal tone is linked to poor mental and attentional regulation, depression, and inflammation and can also evaluate your sensitivity to stress.

Vagus Nerve Treatment Through Acupuncture

Acupuncture has been employed to treat different diseases for over 2000 years. As the title suggests, acupuncture is a medical intervention that involves applying fine needles to certain body areas referred to as acupuncture points or perhaps acupoints.

Acupuncture originated in Asia and, according to all those that use it, facilitates Qi's flow, and that is the life force circulating through our entire body in the form of meridians. Acupoints are presumed to be pathophysiologically associated, reflecting the state of systemic conditions and visceral organs. This is why specific acupoints' stimulation may also evoke a response in the vagus nerve and improve its tone.

Acupuncture stimulation is put on to the acupoint or perhaps a closely affected area for muscle treatment. On the contrary, distal acupuncture stimulation targets diseases present in internal organs, like in the vagus nerve.

Our trained professionals use manual acupuncture to penetrate the skin with a metallic needle and manipulate it by rotating in one or perhaps both directions or perhaps thrusting and lifting.

According to experts, patients may feel a sensation that spreads to other body areas, which is regarded as a useful criterion when evaluating acupuncture's therapeutic efficacy. Based on the reports, acupuncture is a good treatment for many kinds of diseases through its power to regulate inflammatory responses.

Treating the Vagus Nerve Through Mind-Body Therapy

A healthy vagus nerve is in a position to comfortably support your digestive system, which helps regulate sleep patterns and settle nerves. Learning to regulate vagal tone is related to decreased inflammation and a more precise prognosis in individuals suffering from chronic illness, auto-immune disorders, migraines, vagus nerve anxiety, and depression.

Ventral vagal complex, or perhaps VVC, will be the interpersonal communication system in charge of calming and soothing. The social nervous system gets its name since it's liable for your facial expressivity.

Vagal Tone and Heart Rate Variability

Vagal tone is evaluated through the oscillations in heart rate, which occur when we breathe. This is referred to as heart rate variability or HRV. So, your vagus nerve's good tone depends on a minimal rise in heart rate when inhaling and a decline in heart rate when exhaling.

Below, a healthy vagal tone can be regarded as an optimum balance of parasympathetic and sympathetic nervous system actions. In general, individuals with higher HRV can shift better from excitement to relaxation and recover faster from stress.

Tone Your Vagus Nerve

Mind-body therapies are known to manage the vagus nerve and increase resilience through 'safe mobilization and safe immobilization.' This can initially develop your capacity to feel connected, calm, and peaceful. When you've developed a good foundation for accessing your social central nervous system, you can gradually build your tolerance for triggering physiological activation.

Furthermore, mind-body therapy from Jessica will, at the same time, tend to your thoughts, emotional experience, breath, and bodily sensations. Additionally, you can focus on sensing your external environment to recognize your safety in the current moment.

Conclusion

The interaction between the mind and the gut is dependent on a complicated process that includes neural and endocrine, immune, and humoral links.

The vagus nerve is a crucial component of the brain-gut axis. It plays a crucial role in the modulation of inflammation, the maintenance of intestinal homeostasis, and food intake, satiety, and energy homeostasis. Interaction between the vagus nerve and nutrition is known, and vagal tone can influence food intake and weight gain.

Furthermore, the vagus nerve plays a crucial role in the pathogenesis of psychiatric disorders, obesity, and other stress-induced and inflammatory diseases.

Vagus nerve stimulation and many meditation techniques demonstrate that modulating the vagus nerve has a healing effect, primarily due to its relaxing and anti-inflammatory properties.

Extinction paired with VNS is much more rapid compared to extinction paired with sham stimulation. As the FDA now approves it for depression and seizure prevention, VNS is a promising and available readily adjunct to exposure treatment for treating severe anxiety disorders.

Vagus Nerve stimulation is a good anticonvulsant device and has shown in observational studies antidepressant effects in chronic treatment-resistant depression. Because the vagus nerve sends information to brain regions necessary for the stress response (amygdala), hippocampus, insula, orbitofrontal cortex, or LC, this pathway might be involved in sensing manifesting various somatic and cognitive symptoms which characterize stress-related disorders.

Psychotropic drugs, like serotonin reuptake inhibitors, affect both the mind and the gastrointestinal tract and, consequently, should be known as modulators of the brain-gut axis.

Research investigating the interaction between nutritional factors, somatic factors, like heart rate, pharmacological and psychological treatments, and vagal activity has the potential to result in integrative treatment options that incorporate VNS, nutritional approaches, drugs, and psychological interventions, like mindfulness-based approaches, which may be customized to the requirements of the individual patient.

Sharon Copeland

Want more?

Grab My Book "Back to Self-Care FOR FREE in the following page" – Limited Copies Available

This is Not the End

Hi there!

Congratulations! You just reached the end of the book!

You digested a lot of information about the topic and I really hope you discovered something new and inspiring!

You know what comes next. :)

Well, besides leaving a review on the book at the link below, I've shared the link to the FREE BOOK so that you can keep on reading! That's why "This is Not the End."

>>You can Leave a Review Here<<
https://swiy.io/VagusNerveReviewAMZ

If you have any feedback, please get in touch with me at the following contacts, I have them at the beginning of the book, but for your convenience, I've dropped them here too!

Website: sharoncopeland.com

Email: info@sharoncopeland.com

Facebook Page: https://swiy.io/SharonCopelandFBPage

Facebook Support Book:
https://swiy.io/SharonCopelandFBGroup

Instagram: @saroncopelandauthor

Free Workbook

To help you take some "me" time and reflect on which actions to take after the reading, I have prepared a workbook with some key questions to ask yourself. I hope this helps!

You can find the workbook at the following link.

https://swiy.io/VagusNerveWorkbookLP

Or Scan This Code With your Phone Camera

Happy Reading!

>> Discover the Secrets of Self-Help, IT'S FREE! <<

https://swiy.io/selfhelpfree

Or Scan This Code With your Phone Camera

Made in the USA
Las Vegas, NV
17 January 2021